THE MORAL SEX

Woman's Nature in the French Enlightenment

LIESELOTTE STEINBRÜGGE

Translated by Pamela E. Selwyn

New York   Oxford
OXFORD UNIVERSITY PRESS
1995

Oxford University Press

Oxford   New York
Athens   Auckland   Bangkok   Bombay
Calcutta   Cape Town   Dar es Salaam   Delhi
Florence   Hong Kong   Istanbul   Karachi
Kuala Lumpur   Madras   Madrid   Melbourne
Mexico City   Nairobi   Paris   Singapore
Taipei   Tokyo   Toronto

and associated companies in
Berlin   Ibadan

Copyright © 1992 by J. B. Metzler Verlagsbuchhandlung
Original German-language edition: Lieselotte Steinbrügge,
*Das moralische Geschlecht: Theorien und literarische Entwürfe
über die Natur der Frau in der französischen Aufklärung.*
2nd ed., 1992, published by J. B. Metzlersche Verlagsbuchhandlung, Stuttgart,
Germany.

English edition copyright © 1995 by Oxford University Press, Inc.

Published by Oxford University Press, Inc.
198 Madison Avenue, New York, New York 10016

Oxford is a registered trademark of Oxford University Press

Library of Congress Cataloging-in-Publication Data
Steinbrügge, Lieselotte, 1953–
[Das moralische Geschlecht. English]
The moral sex : woman's nature in the French Enlightenment /
Lieselotte Steinbrügge : translated by Pamela E. Selwyn.
p.   cm. Includes bibliographical references
ISBN 0-19-509492-1 (cl.). –ISBN 0-19-509493-X (pbk.)
1. Women–Psychology–History–18th century.
2. Women in literature–France–History–18th century.
3. Women–France–Conduct of life–History–18th century.
I. Title.
HQ1210.S7413   1995   305.4'0944–dc20   94-39210

1 3 5 7 9 8 6 4 2

Printed in the United States of America
on acid-free paper

For Johannes

Preface

Research on the European Enlightenment has had a long and worthy tradition. Until recently, however, studies of gender relations were all but foreign to the republic of letters of the *dix-huitièmistes*. The institutionalization of gender studies at American universities has been a major factor in changing this situation, such that research on the Enlightenment now regularly incorporates questions of gender. One may say without exaggeration that a discussion has now been set in motion that questions old certainties, allowing the age of Enlightenment to appear in a new light. This book, which first appeared in German in 1987, seeks to make a contribution to this discussion.

The bibliography was expanded and updated for the English-language edition by Pamela Selwyn, and the translation was funded by the Free University, Berlin. I would particularly like to thank Hella Tiedemann, Hans Ulrich Gumbrecht, and Johannes Rohbeck, without whose support the original version of this book would never have seen the light of day.

Berlin   L.S.
July 1994

Contents

Introduction　　　　　　　　　　　　　　　　　　　**3**

1. Reason Has No Sex　　　　　　　　　　　　　　　**10**

The Rationalist Tradition of the *Querelle des Femmes*
　(Poulain de la Barre), *11*
Eighteenth-Century Discussions of the
　　Ideal of the Learned Woman
　(Florent de Puisieux, Dom Philippe-Joseph
　Caffiaux, Mademoiselle Archambault), *13*
Emotionalizing the Female Mind
　(Madame de Lambert), *18*

**2. Dividing the Human Race: The Anthropological
　Definition of Woman in the *Encyclopédie***　　　**21**

The Human Being as Natural Being, *21*
The Image of the Useful Human Being:
　Honnêteté Turns Bourgeois, *24*
Woman as Natural Being in the Physiocrats' *Ordre Naturel*, *25*
The Other Side of the Natural Order, *28*
The Moral Sex, *30*

3. The Sensualist Turning Point
　(*Antoine-Léonard Thomas and Pierre Roussel*)　　**35**

4. The Sexualization of Female Existence   **41**

Medical Discourse, *41*
Literary Discourse
   (Denis Diderot), *44*

**5. The Historical and Moral-Philosophical
   Dimensions of the Feminine**
   (*Jean-Jacques Rousseau*)   **54**

Control Over the Passions as Educational
   Objective in *Emile*, *56*
Egoism as the Competitive Society's Ruling Passion
   in the *Discours sur l'origine et les fondements de l'inégalité
   parmi les hommes*, *60*
The History of Female Reason: The Golden Age
   in One's Own Home, *63*
The Return of the Golden Age in *La Nouvelle Héloïse*, *70*
The Function of the Feminine in the Utopia of *Clarens*, *77*

6. The Female Reduced to Natural Instinct
   (*Choderlos de Laclos*)   **83**

7. Female Sensibility   **90**

Rousseau for Everywoman: The Dual Nature
   of the Passions, *90*
The Limited Scope of Female Sensibility, *97*
Raising Girls to Be Society's Moral Conscience:
   Women's Pedagogical Writings
   (Madame de Miremont, Madame Espinassy,
   Madame d'Epinay), *99*

Conclusion   **105**

Notes   *109*
Bibliography   *145*
Index   *155*

THE MORAL SEX

Introduction

Legend has it that in France the eighteenth century was the century of women, and the facts would seem to substantiate this view. The intellectual elite met in salons led by women; the important thinkers of the age corresponded and discussed their ideas with women. A number of women took up writing themselves, producing scientific tracts, translations, novels, or pedagogical programs.[1] Women such as Madame du Châtelet, Madame de Graffigny, Madame Riccoboni, Madame de Lambert, Julie de Lespinasse, and Madame de Genlis—to name only a few—represent this development. It was this integration of women into intellectual life which, a century later, moved the Goncourt brothers to devote a celebrated study to the women of the eighteenth century, in which they concluded that woman had been the governing principle of the age,[2] a topos which has persisted virtually unbroken to this day.[3]

The reasons for this persistence seem to me to lie not so much in the—at least initially convincing—power of facts but rather in the very logic of Enlightenment philosophy. Indeed, the philosophe's aspirations toward emancipation and education did not stop with women. The eighteenth century was an era of upheaval in which human nature, and with it the nature of men and women, was being rethought. The religious worldview was losing its validity, and with it the biblical curse which for centuries had allowed women to be conceived as subordinate to men. The bourgeois notion of natural human equality also facilitated a new anthropological definition of the female human being. "Woman in a state of nature, like man, is a free and powerful being," wrote Choderlos de Laclos

3

in *Des femmes et de leur éducation* (On Women and Their Education),[4] following Rousseau's postulate on the natural equality of all human beings.

This development, however, by no means culminated in the concept of the equality of the sexes. The eighteenth century is the period when the sex-specific character[5] attributed to men and women developed and diverged; it is the epoch in which the ideological and institutional foundations were laid for women's exclusion from civil rights and higher education—in short, from public life. It is the age that saw the emergence of an image of female nature that allowed precisely these exclusions to be considered "natural."

Historians, particularly those studying the history of the family, have outlined the sociohistorical factors underpinning this development.[6] The exigencies of the bourgeois system of production accorded the family a purely reproductive role. Women were relegated to work that, lying as it did outside the sphere of social production, did not allow them to participate in scientific-technological progress and thus demanded of them other qualities than those required there. At the same time, the physiocrats, for whom population growth represented the fundamental precondition for all economic progress, glorified the maternal virtues in a sort of large-scale advertising campaign aimed at reminding women of their demographic duties.[7] Finally, the recognition of children as people in their own right also contributed to a new understanding of the maternal role.[8]

All these factors belonging to the realm of social history and the history of mentalities are the premises upon which my analyses rest. I assume that the theories and literary representations of woman's nature I discuss cannot be explained without these actual historical factors. They do not, however, provide the ultimate explanation. Rather, they demarcate the tension between, on the one hand, the Enlightenment aspiration to emancipate a (female) sex maintained in ignorance and, on the other, the "objective necessities" of the bourgeois economic order, which required women to adopt the role of housewife and mother. What interests me is *how* this tension, within which the recasting of female identity occurred, could be resolved theoretically in order that the concept of a general female incapacity for human emancipation could become a universal anthropological truth.

This concept, which can still be encountered today,[9] is by no means a product of the counter-Enlightenment. The division of humanity into two unequal parts was legitimated with genuinely Enlightenment principles—

this in an age professing devotion to the equality of all human beings. [7] The road there led past the very authority that allowed men to conceive of liberation from the shackles of tutelage: Nature. The feminist dialectic of Enlightenment shows that the idea of (human) nature, the paradigm of Enlightenment emancipation in general, when applied to women, comes to mean "subsumption" and "limitation." My task in what follows is to sketch the path this process took.

The question of woman's nature greatly exercized thinkers of the time. It was the object of medical, historiographic, anthropological, philosophical, and, not least, literary discourse. The *querelle des femmes*, that debate over the question of the equality of the sexes which had been raging at least since the *Roman de la rose*, had revived, particularly since the 1750s.[10] This discussion was multifaceted, encompassing nearly all aspects of female existence, from woman's social role to her biological nature and sexuality.[11] The aspect that particularly interests me here is the problem of women's intellectual capacity and the related ideal of the learned woman.

This aspect seems significant to me for two reasons. First, in an age in which the belief in progress was expressed as belief in the transformative power of reason, the way in which women's intellectual capacity was evaluated was a decisive determinant of their position within the culture. Second, it can be demonstrated that the alteration in the period's ideal of femininity occurred in express rejection of a female type primarily defined by active participation in intellectual life.

Poulain de la Barre's 1673 pamphlet *De l'égalité des deux sexes* (On the Equality of the Two Sexes), the first detailed examination of the theme of female intellect, broke ground for the Enlightenment *querelle*. Thus, it is no coincidence that virtually all of the polemics that were to follow addressed his arguments, either implicitly or explicitly. For this reason, I treat the writings of Caffiaux, Archambault, Puisieux, and de Lambert, which exemplify this discussion, chiefly from the standpoint of women's intellectual capacity (chapter 1).

The form this discussion took can, I believe, only be understood against the background of the period's philosophical anthropology, as I try to show in chapter 3. Research into the organic preconditions of human knowledge also set a precedent for the medical and philosophical discourse on women and was fundamental for the recasting of ideas of female nature. The reevaluation of the female body took on particular significance in this context. Argumentation in terms of sensory physiology at first facilitated the liberation of woman from the myths surrounding her corpo- reality, allowing for the emancipatory "mobilization" of nature against repressive superstition. On the other hand, it was precisely the great sig- nificance attributed to woman's physical nature that, in conjunction with physiocratic discourse, led to an unprecedented reduction of woman to the creatural. It was this final aspect that was to become ideologically domi- nant. Using texts from the *Encyclopédie* and by Thomas and Roussel, I try to show that at the end of the age of Enlightenment, the woman who emerged from reflexions about female nature was not a full individual but a being viewed solely in terms of her sex (chapters 2 and 3).

The Enlightenment debate was by no means limited to a dismantling of woman's human—particularly intellectual—capabilities, which at first made women appear as deficient men. Rather, this reduction was accom- panied by a broadened anthropological definition of woman's sex-specific character, which was based precisely on woman's supposed closeness to nature. My central thesis here is that the accentuation of creaturliness, and thus also of emotionality, over enlightened rationality predestined women to adopt a particular role. The exclusion of women from public life and its complement, their relegation to private life, appeared to qualify women particularly for the realm of *morality*, conceived of in bourgeois society as a genuinely private morality, and one that could only be socially efficacious through the private sphere. And because this morality achieved an increasingly emotional basis in the age of Enlightenment, not least because of its private character, female nature could be proclaimed as particularly competent as emotional morality. With this, the definition of woman as "the sex" sealed women's destiny as the moral authority of a society that excluded certain direct human emotions from public inter- actions. Woman became *the moral sex*. Humane qualities survived (only) as a female principle.

It is this aspect of the *querelle* which I will use to show that with the standardization of female nature—that is, its subjection to strict and uni- form norms—more was at stake than merely the "battle of the sexes." What is at stake here is not simply "woman" but the place of compassion in a society whose economic reproduction rested on the "war of all against all." The function of a moral authority, an unfilled position in the mas- culine world of business, is fulfilled by woman, who appears predestined for this role by virtue of biological propensities which place her closer than man to the sphere of compassion.

This "construction" could not stand up to reality, though, and the feelings that supposedly hibernated in the warm niches of family life, far from the rigors of bourgeois rationality, did not survive unscathed: a bitter experience not only for women. Woman as the sustainer of humane qualities continued to exist, in her pure form, mostly in fiction, as Virginia Woolf acutely observed: "Imaginatively she is of the highest importance; practically she is completely insignificant. . . . Some of the most inspired words, some of the most profound thoughts in literature fall from her lips; in real life she could hardly read, could scarcely spell, and was the property of her husband."[12] For this reason, I have used the ideal-typical literary models of femininity developed by two significant eighteenth-century writers to trace the "idea of woman's nature" against the background of the theoretical writings discussed in earlier chapters (chapters 4 and 5). Rousseau and Diderot seemed appropriate for several reasons. Their works represent two stages (in the systematic, not the chronological, sense) in the redefinition of woman's nature. Diderot remains at the first stage of development of sex character—the demotion of the female human being to a sexual being. Julie in Rousseau's *La Nouvelle Héloïse* is a much more complex character than the Tahitian "savages" in the *Supplément au voyage de Bougainville* or the figure of Suzanne Simonin in *La Religieuse* (The Nun). She embodies just that moral authority of the "female principle" in the sense of the functions I described. The reasons for these differing models of femininity do not lie, as might appear at first glance, in the authors' divergent biographies or in their personal tastes. To avoid falling into crude reductionism, one must examine them in the context of the authors' anthropological conceptions.

It was Rousseau's position that gained the widest influence. I have followed its "popularization" in some broadly distributed eighteenth-century works (chapter 6). These contributed significantly to the entry into collective consciousness of the construction of female sex-specific character as a natural fact and thus as an anthropological constant.

Texts in many scholarly disciplines and literary genres took up the discussion of female nature. For this reason, I have chosen to examine works from various fields and levels of theorization.[13] Up until now, only Paul Hoffmann has devoted extensive and detailed consideration to the majority of these discourses. His book *La Femme dans la pensée des Lumières* (Woman in Enlightenment Thought) examines almost the entirety of eighteenth-century literature. The methodological approach of his monograph appears problematic, however. Hoffmann starts from the assumption that the discourse about woman cannot be analyzed rationally using either immanent logic or an examination of external reasons. "Neither logical nor sociological causality can explain the evolution of ideas about woman. The sum of the discourses which sketch its fleeting and eternal face at every period of history could never add up to a science."[14] Thus Hoffmann denies the possibility that the discourses about woman might have the status of scholarly theories and, with it, the possibility of a scholarly analysis of the texts' contents. This denial also leads to a doubling of the discourse on woman. Here he influences his own interpretation. It is no accident that Hoffmann refers to Diderot's *Sur les femmes* (On Women) and adopts for his own study Diderot's generalization that one cannot discuss women objectively. According to Hoffmann, fantasies and "factual statements" about women's nature resist critical analysis, allowing instead for merely subjective evaluations: "We admit our partiality! But the object of our investigation forbade any objectivity. No one can speak of woman without becoming involved, without compromising himself."[15]

This attitude is symptomatic of a (male-dominated) scholarly discourse on women which accepts uncritically the characteristics attributed to women, adopting them as the starting point for its investigations. Hoffmann's certainty that all discourses on woman are, of necessity, incoherent, changeable, vague, and subjective rests on the unspoken (because so widely shared) attitude that these are precisely some of the characteristics of women's nature.

Throughout his study, Hoffman treats sex-specific character as a valid anthropological given. "At no moment does woman's freedom appear more problematic than when she is called, by her own nature, to bear a child and bring it into the world. At no moment is the body more sovereign, but there is also no more propitious occasion for reason to demonstrate her duties and capabilities."[16] This approach appears methodologically questionable because Hoffmann takes as his starting point ideas which were the *result* of developments during the eighteenth century. Whether it was a woman's duty to bear children, and whether this duty restricted her freedom, was precisely one of the issues at stake in the *querelle*. Hoffmann's own assumptions preclude his grasping this evolution.

In order to do justice to the different types of texts, I have treated the various genres separately. Only in this way could I account for the peculiarities of the texts, particularly the differences between fictional, philosophical, and popular-scientific literature. At the same time, this classification did not determine the substantive methodology of my work. Rather, I selected texts for analysis primarily according to the central theoretical issues just sketched. For example, my reading of Diderot's literary texts is informed by questions which emerged from my study of the scientific paradigms and medical presuppositions underpinning the debate on women's nature. I selected the theoretical texts according to representativeness. Here, in particular, there is a multitude of texts to choose from, which I did not need to treat exhaustively since, at a certain level, they all make the same arguments. For this reason, I have chosen to treat a few exemplary texts that display typical discursive strategies regarding the questions that interested me.

1

Reason Has No Sex

In the middle of the eighteenth century, the question of the equality of the sexes became a controversial topic of discussion. The emancipatory Enlightenment movement also shook up traditional ideals of womanhood. Proponents of theories of sexual equality could look to a famous predecessor who had already made a vigorous contribution to the *querelle des femmes* in the seventeenth century: François Poulain de la Barre. Two works by Florent de Puisieux and Dom Philippe Caffiaux,[1] which appeared in the mid-eighteenth century, stand in a direct line with Poulain's famous 1673 pamphlet *De l'égalité des deux sexes* (On the Equality of the Two Sexes). In order to understand the peculiarities of the late-Enlightenment *querelle*, we must first look at this work.

De l'égalité des deux sexes can be regarded as a milestone in debates on the equality of the sexes. As a Cartesian, Poulain de la Barre attempts to deduce the equality of man and woman *systematically*. In so doing, he opposes not only the proponents of female inferiority but also the approaches of earlier and contemporary apologists of the female sex.

Ever since the Renaissance, the chief interest of women's defenders had been to free them from the onus of sinfulness bestowed by the medieval church. The propagation of courtly platonic love, for example, as expressed in the writings of Christine de Pizan, Marguerite de Navarre, and Louise Labé,[2] among others, reflected the aspirations of "feminists" at the time to accord woman a role other than that of man's subordinate. The advocates of improving women's lot sought to demonstrate women's virtues and achievements with examples taken from throughout history, mythology, and religion, and this prolific literary tradition lived on into the eighteenth century.[3]

All of these writings take the same approach: Using an endlessly repetitive sequence of examples, the authors try to build a positive image of woman. They simply order the "empirical" material, citing so many concrete examples of abstract characteristics intended to demonstrate the equality or even the superiority of women that the sheer mass of exemplary cases render plausible their preconceived ideas.[4] An author, for example, who wanted to show that women also could be stalwart and brave would list all the battles fought by Amazons, from antiquity to Joan of Arc.[5] In time, a sort of canon of heroic female exploits emerged which persisted into the eighteenth century. One can call this approach apologetic because the qualities claimed for women were not grounded in argument but merely presumed and justified by a random selection of mere facts. The choice of examples points to a changed interpretation of written tradition, particularly of the bible. For example, whereas the creation of Eve from Adam's rib had previously been cited as proof of woman's second-class status, it was now cited as evidence of her greater perfection because it showed that Eve was not made of mere earth. In the end, the legitimation for the positive image of women consisted merely in a revaluation of literary tradition, using the same methods as its opponents.

The Rationalist Tradition of the *Querelle des Femmes*

Poulain de la Barre's aforementioned brochure takes defenses of the "Cause des femmes" in a new direction. Dispensing with compilations of heroic deeds, he proceeds instead—like Descartes—to subject all previous arguments for female inferiority to methodological doubt. In his view, the fact that women are represented neither in the arts, nor the sciences, nor in public office by no means demonstrates that they were unfit for these *by nature*. Those who draw this conclusion are allowing themselves to be led by prejudice: "[W]e are filled with prejudices, and . . . we must renounce them completely if we are to attain clear and definite knowledge."[6] He rejects the uncritical adoption of received facts which prevents us from penetrating to the heart of the matter.

Following this methodological principle, Poulain next attempts to define woman's "true nature." In the Cartesian tradition it is the intellect that is central and that becomes the touchstone of equality. Descartes had said, after all, that "common sense is the best distributed thing in the world."[7] Although Descartes was claiming the essential equal capacity for reason in the service of a sociopolitical opposition to feudal hierarchies, without taking gender into account, he at least created the epistemological preconditions for asserting the intellectual equality of the sexes. Poulain de la Barre takes up this premise, creating out of it arguments which were to point the way for further debate. If common sense, or reason, was really equally distributed among human beings, then this must hold true for women as well.[8]

A second, decisive argument proceeds from the Cartesian separation between *res cognitans* and *res extensa*. Because reason is separated from the body, physical traits exercise no direct influence over cognition. As a result, the specific qualities of the female body do not influence women's thought, just as the bodily distinctions between the sexes more generally are of no significance. "Reason has no sex" (l'esprit n'a point de sexe)[9]—with this famous phrase, which unites the two arguments, Poulain de la Barre radicalized the Enlightenment postulate of equality by applying it to relations between men and women.

Such deductions leave women's actual subordination untouched. Why is it that women, who are by nature possessed of the same rational capacities as men, do not participate in men's achievements? In order to answer this question, Poulain refers to history—not in the style of the compilers, but rather by means of a genetic-reconstructive method. Having already explored woman's true nature, Poulain must now seek out the causes of her inequality in history. In the savage state, man and woman were "simple and innocent," doing the same work (hunting and agriculture) and neither had dominion over the other. The origins of inequality, Poulain de la Barre believed, must be sought in men's first usurpations of power. Here right, not reason, made might. Women did not share men's thirst for power. Since that time, men had succeeded in oppressing them. "[T]hey [women] were subordinated solely by the rule of force, and it was neither a lack of natural ability nor of merit that prevented them from participating in all that which raises our sex over theirs."[10] With the passage of time, the result of relations of force came to appear as women's natural characteristics.

The principle of equality, arrived at by deduction, is the precondition for a pedagogical concept which allows women the same opportunities as men, particularly to engage in scholarship. Poulain de la Barre develops this concept in a programmatic work published a year later, *De l'éducation des dames pour la conduite de l'esprit dans les sciences et dans les mœurs* (On the Education of Ladies for the Application of Their Minds to Scholarship and Manners). In the preface he elucidates the title, noting that the work consists of conversations with a lady desiring to devote herself to scholarly endeavors. The principles he sets down, however, may be equally useful for men, "as there is only one method for instructing both, since they belong to the same species."[11]

Poulain de la Barre was the first author to have developed a pedagogical program for women conceived neither in terms of male/universalist educational principles, nor as complementary to them, but rather in terms of the equal capabilities of the two sexes. His aim was to champion rational thinking over dogmatic-scholastic pedagogy. "The principal and most important maxim of all is to instill in men, as far as possible, that sovereign reason which enables them to judge all things sensibly and without prejudice."[12] "Men" (*hommes*) here definitely refers to both genders and explicitly includes the female segment of humanity. The quality of this universal human nature must be derived from principles. History, once cited as proof of female capacities and incapacities, no longer explains relations between the sexes. Rather, history consists merely of a sequence of accidental events without inner cohesion; concrete history actually falsifies the true nature of woman, whose abilities were expressed differently under changing circumstances. From then on, it became standard scholarly practice in the *querelle des femmes* to disregard these historical circumstances and attribute female nature to immutable principles.

Eighteenth-Century Discussions of the Ideal of the Learned Woman

Poulain de la Barre's thesis of "the sexless mind" was expressed pointedly in eighteenth-century discussions of women's role in the sciences. In 1750 a brochure appeared with the programmatic title *La Femme n'est pas inférieure à l'homme* (Woman Is Not Inferior to Man). Florent de Puisieux, under whose name the work appeared, claims in the preface that he was only its translator and that the author was an Englishwoman.[13] Without naming the source, the work contains some passages lifted directly from Poulain de la Barre's pamphlet.

The author argues against the practice of denying women other abilities because of their biological capacity to bear children.[14] She anticipates the objection that it is, after all, women's duty to serve men. It is precisely this assumption which she rejects, even if all appearances in daily life appear to support it. Like Poulain de la Barre, she considers it methodologically untenable to portray women's "disadvantages"— the results of men's "unjust usurpations" (*usurpations injustes*) and "tyranny"—as eternal characteristics of female nature. "[T]hey [men] are so accustomed to seeing matters as they are today that they cannot imagine them ever being otherwise."[15] In her unbiased treatment of the problem, she resists making the specificity of the female body women's dominant characteristic. "It is common knowledge that the difference between the sexes is purely physical, and restricted to those parts of the body serving the propagation of human nature."[16] Reason has no sex and, as a consequence, cognition is the same in both sexes. The demonstration of this assertion forms the centerpiece of her treatise. It is no accident that the longest section of her text is chapter 6, which asks, "Whether or not women are naturally capable of teaching the sciences." (Si les femmes sont naturellement capables d'enseigner les sciences ou non)[17] It is, after all, the issue of women's intellectual capacity which initially dominated Enlightenment discussions of women's nature.

It is surprising that mental abilities became the central criterion for sexual equality. How much more obvious it would have been to invoke women's physical weakness to prove their unfitness for activities requiring strength, such as artisanal labor, and to use this deficiency as an argument for their general inferiority. Such arguments are virtually absent from the text under discussion here, however. Our author expends little energy refuting such claims, merely asserting briefly that among women, as among men, there were strong and weak individuals; those who do not believe this need only watch poor rural women engaging in heavy agricultural labor.[18]

This explanation, which may appear surprising today, was generally accepted in the eighteenth century. Even proponents of the notion of male superiority did not justify women's subordination with arguments about their unfitness for particular activities requiring physical strength. Instead, they merely used the peculiarities of female anatomy as the occasion for claiming that women were *intellectually* and *morally* inferior.

There seem to be two essential supports for this line of argumentation. One was the power of fact. Women indeed worked as hard as men in agriculture, which at the time employed five-sixths of the female population.[19] In some regions, according to local custom, women even did the heaviest labor. In some cases they replaced draught animals in the fields. The division of work into light and heavy physical labor by no means followed gender lines. The same can be said of the artisanal trades and emerging industry.[20] Women's integration in the agricultural and artisanal production processes was so obvious as to make it unthinkable for any *homme de lettres*, no matter how convinced of female inferiority, to endure the same physical rigors that were the everyday lives of peasant women or artisan's wives.

On the other hand, in an age marked by faith in reason's power to shape history, only intellectual capacity counted as a criterion for "classifying" woman. The significance accorded to reason in the emancipation of humanity led to a revalorization of intellectual labor. It was also in this period that the figure of the professional scholar emerged. Scholarly work was no longer conducted chiefly as a private hobby in one's own study but was institutionalized in academies.[21] It is thus only logical that the debate should have been conducted in the field of intellectual equality.

For the author translated by Puisieux, the assertion that reason has no sex is the position from which she can proceed to refute the inferiority of her own sex. One after the other, she reviews various disciplines (rhetoric, jurisprudence, medicine, theology, philosophy), concluding in each case that women are just as well suited to practice them as men. Even the exercise of the "art of war" is, in her estimation, primarily intellectual labor, and thus well within women's capacities: "[A] woman is just as capable as a man of learning, with the aid of maps, about good and bad routes, safe or unsafe roads and suitable places to set up camp. What is to prevent her from gaining knowledge of all the stratagems of war, the means of charging the enemy, organizing a retreat, planning a surprise attack, laying an ambush."[22] With her demand for the admittance of women to all public offices,[23] Puisieux's author makes it clear that hers is not merely a general appeal for better female education. She calls for a professional attitude toward scholarship and explicitly disapproves of a fashionable smattering of learning. She sets "true knowledge" (*vrai scavoir*) and "thorough knowledge" (*les connoissances solides*) against "superficial knowledge" (*scavoir superficiel*).[24]

Women must be judged by reason alone, which must prove itself both in the sciences and in public social life. The elevation of the learned woman to a female ideal constitutes, in the tradition of Poulain de la Barre, the centerpiece of rationalist argumentation in the *querelle des femmes*, signaling a break with received prejudices and myths about female nature.

Dom Philippe-Joseph Caffiaux's *Défenses du Beau Sexe, ou Mémoires historiques, philosophiques et critiques pour servir d'Apologie aux femmes* (Defenses of the Fair Sex, or A Historical, Philosophical, and Critical Treatise in the Form of a Vindication of Women),[25] published three years later in 1753, also propagates the model of the learned woman. The author explicitly places himself in the tradition of Poulain de la Barre. He begins his preface with "M. Poulain's Thoughts on this Subject" and cites his authority with liberal quotations. Caffiaux, whose voluminous and sometimes repetitive book claims to bring together all the topoi of traditional defenses of women, does not fail to enumerate the examples handed down from classical mythology, the Bible, and historiography in order to lend more weight to his revalorization of the female sex, and in so doing he joins the ranks of the sixteenth- and seventeenth-century *compilateurs*. The first fifty pages of his second volume, for example, are devoted to the "heroic and illustrious deeds by means of which women have secured immortality" (Actions héroiques & éclatantes par où les femmes ont eternisé leur mémoire). His accounts of the heroic deeds of learned women, however, are even more extensive. The book's 200-page-long fifth chapter is entitled "On the Progress Which Women Have Made in All the Sciences" (Du progrès que les femmes ont fait dans toutes les sciences),[26] thus integrating women into a question which exercised the minds of leading thinkers of the age from Fontenelle to Turgot and Condorcet. Their attempt to reconstruct historical progress via the progress of the human intellect formed the core of Enlightenment theories of history.[27] In according the female intellect its place in this progress, Caffiaux brings women into historiography as historical subjects.

Poulain de la Barre and his successor Puisieux had already accused men of appropriating women's scholarship and, by extension, their historicity as well. Caffiaux also describes the exclusion of women from scholarly endeavor as an act of force: "How men seized science" (Comment les hommes se sont emparés de la science).[28] His gallery of learned women is vivid evidence of how levels of argument in the *querelle des femmes* had shifted from the seventeenth to the eighteenth century. Heroic deeds in the service of "King and country" or to "defend or avenge their honor,"[29] borrowed from the chivalric moral code and the traditional canon of female apologia, are by no means absent from the book, but they now take second place to the ideal of professional learning. Caffiaux knows that only the list of female philosophers, theologians, rhetoricians, poets, philologists, mathematicians, physicians, artists, and academicians has any hope of entering the annals of history. Abstracting from women's actual opportunities, Caffiaux legitimates the concept of egalitarian gender relations here by claiming women's participation in the progress of scholarship.

This contribution to the "progress of reason" is presented as proof of woman's rationality. What marks the human being is no longer the mere possession of intellect; he or she must consistently work at perfecting it. Only when it can be shown that women have participated in the development of the sciences—so essential to the progress of human history— can women's fundamental fitness for scholarship be demonstrated. This dimension of late-Enlightenment historical theory revalorizes historical example, which no longer appears in the form of catalogues of random incidents but, rather, as the historical unfolding of a natural principle. For Caffiaux, history is the place where the true nature of woman as a rational being equal to man is both expressed and put to the test.

The debate between Mademoiselle Archambault and two anonymous male opponents, published in Paris in 1750 as *Dissertation sur la question lequel de l'homme ou de la femme est plus capable de constance . . .* (Dissertation on the Question, Whether Man or Woman Is More Capable of Constancy . . .), also revolves around the question of women's fitness for scholarly endeavor.[30] The two gentlemen deny that women possess the requisite *constance*, by which they mean perseverance and tenacity as well as courage and self-conquest. Archambault insists on the separation of body and mind, emphasizing that "woman's weakness and fragility may only be applied to her body, just as man's superior strength only extends to his."[31] In contrast to the polemics treated up until now, however, she does not proceed from gender-neutral reason. Instead, she attributes to the female intellect superior qualities, bestowed by God in compensation for women's lesser physical strength. "[T]hey [women] have better memories, more receptive, lively and penetrating minds than most men, as even their enemies maintain; they possess better and surer taste and more discerning judgment of the fine and the delicate."[32] Archambault's opponent M.L.L.R. by no means denies women the typical qualities she sets out. Indeed, he substantiates them, owning that women are better novelists than men because of the *délicatesse* of their style and the tenderness of their sentiments. However, he confidently opposes the postulate of female superiority, asking "[D]o they [novels] suffice to entitle women to call themselves learned?"[33] He answers firmly in the negative, arguing that women lack the "reliable reason, the breadth of mind and acuity of judgment" needed to engage in mathematics and the natural sciences, to rise to metaphysical speculation, and to develop sound moral principles.[34] This, he continues, is no reason to look down on women, however. It is, rather, a reason to admire them: "[A] woman who does what she can in her own sphere, who watches over her servants, lays the first groundwork of her children's education, keeps her house in order and obeys her husband, deserves as much praise as all these heroes, great statesmen and scholars."[35] Relegating women to the family sphere is nothing new. At the end of the seventeenth century—not least in reaction to Poulain de la Barre—Fénelon was already polemicizing vehemently against learned women, developing a pedagogical program for girls centered around household management which was to become the bible of Madame de Maintenon's girls' school at Saint-Cyr.[36] This attitude came under increasing fire in the eighteenth century, as champions of the women's cause, both male and female, adopted the Enlightenment postulate of equality and supported their right to participate in human progress not only with enlightened argument but also often with their own practice as learned women. At the same time, the role of wife and mother meshed precisely with the socioeconomic needs of the middle classes.

The Enlightenment's understanding of itself, on the one hand, and the objective constraints of social conditions, on the other, led to a change in the *querelle des femmes* in the middle of the eighteenth century; one already hinted at in the debate between Archambault and her opponents: women's equality was no longer understood as an equality of identical capabilities, but rather as one of *different* but equally valuable natures.

Emotionalizing the Female Mind

This change had already been anticipated by the opposing side, however. Madame de Lambert, whose *Réflexions nouvelles sur les femmes* (New Reflections on Women)[37] carried on Poulain de la Barre's postulate of equality, had already began to make gender-specific differentiations within this concept.

Women, Lambert argues, are commonly said to have more *goût* (taste) than men. She gladly accepts this "gift which men present to ladies,"[38] insisting, however, that *goût* is not merely a matter of feeling but also of knowledge arrived at by reason. "I believe that taste depends upon two things: the fine feelings of the heart and great acuity of the mind."[39] Lambert's attempt to turn the weaknesses attributed to women into strengths shows that women's better judgment in matters of taste is by no means coupled with an incapacity for rational thought. Women had been unjustly accused of judging only with their hearts, and not their minds. Feeling might dominate, but it did not prevent women from arriving at clear understanding. Lambert was not prepared to accept the denigration of *sentiment*. In women, sentiment did not combat reason but rather led, almost naturally, to reason: "[I]n women, thoughts come of their own accord, and are put in order more by sentiment than by reflexion: Nature reasons for them, sparing them all effort."[40] Thus, female reason is, in the end, superior to male reason: "[N]othing is so absolute as the intellectual superiority arising from the capacity to feel."[41]

Lambert thus boldly demands woman's right to recognition of her intellectual contributions. As an author who did not dare to publish her own works for fear of offending against propriety (*bienséance*), she stressed the significance of societal approval of women's intellectual development. "Glory, the soul and pillar of all intellectual achievement, is denied them."[42] That sounds more courageous than the practical advice to her daughter published before the *Réflexions*.[43] While in the *Avis d'une mère a son fils* (A Mother's Advice to Her Son) the son is admonished to be proud, confident, and ambitious in order to attain fame,[44] the daughter's wings are clipped: "Your greatest ornament is modesty."[45]

The education proposed for girls is appropriately mediocre. A bit of history, philosophy, and ethics; Latin, because it is the language of the Church. Italian, "the language of love," has already been rejected as too dangerous.[46] For the same reason she recommends that daughters not read novels. Scholarship is a vice against which the daughter must be on guard: "[R]emember that girls should approach the sciences with almost the same delicate modesty as they approach the vices."[47]

Seen against the background of these two *Avis,* formulated separately for sons and daughters, Renate Baader's assessment, placing Madame de Lambert in the tradition of Poulain de la Barre, is accurate only in part.[48] All the criticism of the neglect of girls' education in the *Réflexions* should not blind us to the fact that Lambert falls short of previous demands, and that in her *Avis* to her daughter she scarcely undertakes "all possible efforts to develop and improve female education."[49] Baader's assessment is correct in that Lambert does not yet place any limitations on female reason. Above all, she addresses herself in general to any attempt to denigrate women.

At the same time, though, Lambert introduces a differentiation between the sexes that would have been unthinkable for proponents of radical equality. Man and woman were considered completely equal on the basis of reason. The revalorization of feeling added a new human capacity attributed in unequal proportions to men and women. Through this a new, particularly female, quality arose. Sensitivity and empathy were recast as something specific to women. Even if this actually accorded women more capabilities than previously, the rationalists' postulate of equality had been left behind.

On the other hand, it is precisely Lambert's reinterpretation that appears to vindicate the thesis of the equality of the sexes. Sentiment, newly attributed to women, was not yet regarded as opposed to reason. More sensitivity did not (yet) mean less reason. Empathy did not prevent women from thinking; on the contrary, it enhanced their capacity for understanding. This was only possible because feeling was still considered as spontaneous a capacity of the human *mind* as reason. In this, Lambert differs substantially from later attempts to derive women's particular sensitivity (as opposed to rationality) from physiological factors, whereby women's merely physical feelings were seen as inferior to men's intellectual capabilities. In maintaining the unity of emotionality and rationality, Lambert guarded women against denigration.

Her approach to specifying female qualities nevertheless provided one of the preconditions for a devalorization of women. It was, after all, only the differentiation between the sexes that allowed them to be evaluated differently. Surely, Lambert accorded women a new characteristic, but it was precisely this well-meaning addition that facilitated women's reduction to that selfsame characteristic. The stage was now set for a female anthropology of the Enlightenment. Madame de Lambert is important to the extent that she showed the way to a definition of human nature divided along gender lines. The *Encyclopédie* permits us to study this anthropology in a systematic context.

2

Dividing the Human Race: The Anthropological Definition of Woman in the Encyclopédie

The Human Being as Natural Being

Diderot and d'Alembert's *Encyclopédie*[1] represents an ambitious attempt to collect and make available in systematic form the sum of eighteenth-century knowledge. Anthropology has a central place within this system. A closer look, however, reveals that the definitions it offers of what is "human" apply only to the male half of humanity. This statement may seem merely to repeat a well-known fact, but does this mean that from its very inception the new "science of man" excluded woman as an object of knowledge? In the following chapter I would like to discover whether and *how* woman became a topic apart, and what function she served within the system of Enlightenment anthropology.

The most general definition of the human being can be found under the entry "Man" (HOMME [*Morale*]):

> MAN (*Moral*): This word has no precise meaning, merely reminding us of all that we are; but what we are cannot be contained in a single definition. To show but a part of this requires further divisions and details. We shall not speak here either of our outward form nor of the organic structure that places us in the class of the animals. See MAN (*Anatomy*). The man under consideration here is that being who thinks, wills and acts.[2]

The article undertakes no separate, gender-specific definition of the male human being. French, like English, does not make the distinction (possible in German, for example) between *Mensch* (human being) and *Mann* (male human being), so that *man* is simply subsumed under *Man*.

"Woman", in contrast, is defined in a separate article, "Woman" (FEMME [*Anthropologie*]), as "the female of man".[3] This special status has led Friederike Hassauer-Roos to conclude that woman was no longer to be construed as a human being but rather as something separate, contrasted to the universality of the human and thus excluded from the concept *Man*. As a result, woman's humanity remains vague, and she is not, at least not explicitly, defined as a human being. As a human, she thus represents a "systematic empty space" that functions as an absence to be filled, at best after the fact, by imagination—*outside* the total anthropological system.[4]

Consistent with this analysis, Hassauer-Roos ultimately understands Enlightenment anthropology as the science of *man*. In so doing, however, she misunderstands the nature of eighteenth-century anthropology. The fact that the description "the female of man" only refers to woman in her capacity as a natural being by no means calls into question her anthropological definition. The characterization of human beings as natural and creaturely can even be regarded as a central trait of the *Encyclopédie* and of the anthropology of the later Enlightenment more generally. This becomes clear when we consult further articles on the subject.

In setting out to answer the question "What is a human being?," the Encyclopedists proceed from human beings' natural condition. Even the aforementioned article "Man" (HOMME), which is included in the discipline of *Morale*, indicating that it is devoted to the nonphysical side of human beings, expressly calls attention to the animalistic aspects of human nature. A number of articles on anatomy and natural history treat the biological nature of human beings. The fundamental articles HOMME (*Hist. nat.*) and HOMME (*Anatomie*) by no means use the term *homme* in a gender-*un*specific manner only. To do so would indicate that, in the final analysis, *homme* as male would represent the universally human. In fact, the articles do differentiate on the basis of gender. Despite the fact that in French as in English, *Man* and *man* are homonyms, the two can be clearly differentiated here. In this context, the authors borrow a term usually applied to animals (*mâle*) in order to make clear when they are speaking of men (e.g., in the article HOMME (*Exposition anatomique du corps de l'*).[5]

The *Encyclopédie* thus provides parallel *natural-historical* definitions for female and male human beings. In the minds of Enlightenment thinkers, these definitions are part of an anthropology grounded largely in natural history. They are nothing more than definitions of "the human being," to which species women expressly belong.

It is only in later descriptions that women begin to be set apart from the definition of the human being. The human being is, to be sure, part of nature, but at the same time—in contrast to other natural beings—also its ruler. Asking what distinguishes human beings from animals, and answering in the spirit of the theoreticians of progress, Le Roy cites human inventiveness:

> But all of their [animals'] actions, taken together, still leave an infinite distance between themselves and *man*. Man's dominion over them may have been acquired by illegitimate means, but that nonetheless proves the superiority of his methods and thus of his nature. One cannot help but be struck by this advantage when one regards man's mighty achievements, when one examines in detail his arts and the progress of his sciences, when one sees him traversing the seas, measuring the heavens, and stealing the very noise and effects of thunder.[6]

Specifically, human reason, the ability to transform nature through invention, makes of the human "a being . . . who appears to stand above all the other animals he dominates."[7] These passages no longer differentiate according to gender. In contrast to the anatomical and natural-historical descriptions of the human being, the differences of meaning between *Man* and *man* disappear here. Because one word stands for both, the male human being is implicitly named in the definition of *Homme*, while the female human being implicitly disappears from the definition. There are no analogous definitions under the rubric "Woman" (FEMME). Neither the article FEMME (*Anthropologie*) nor the article FEMME (*Morale*), for example, lists the spirit of invention as a characteristic distinguishing women from animals.

But even these observations should not lead us to conclude that woman's human status was in doubt, that she was excluded from the concept of human being. She was, after all, defined as a human natural being. Her exclusion applies to the human quality of rationality—also implicit here—attributed to man. But just as man does not lose his status as a human natural being, so the purely biological definition of woman does not rob her of humanity. In the minds of the Encyclopedists, the human being was a rational *animal*. That which was specifically human—reason—did not comprise all of human nature.

It was thus not a matter of whether or not women were human beings. The problem, rather, lay in the *divergent* definitions of female and male human beings. Woman's humanity was thus not undefined, but defined *differently* from that of men. Only with this working hypothesis can we uncover the concrete definitions of woman *within* the anthropological system of the *Encyclopédie*.

The following account will examine more closely the internal structure of the concept *Homme*, in order to analyze the respective places occupied by man and woman in Enlightenment anthropology. To do so, it will be necessary to abandon abstract definitions of concepts and to return to the ensemble of discourses in the *Encyclopédie*. I shall not limit myself here to the immanent analysis of concepts; rather, I would like to show, using certain significant examples, why in the minds of the Encyclopedists the specific humanity of woman was not identical to that of man.

The Image of the Useful Human Being: *Honnêteté* Turns Bourgeois

The many articles in the field *Morale* provide us with an idealized image of the human being, whose concrete model character is already expressed by its crystallization into a particular concept—the *honnête homme*. Borrowed from aristocratic usage, it may be understood as a bourgeois rallying cry. One finds this term, virtually a shorthand for all the virtues admired by the Encyclopedists, in almost every fundamental article, but often also in short, definitional ones. The *Encyclopédie* dismantles at every turn the original meaning of this term—as formulated, for example, by the Chevalier de Méré in the seventeenth century as a courtly code of behavior. It is replaced by the bourgeois-enlightened meaning of *honnêteté*, the diametrical opposite of the aristocratic notion.[8]

I shall limit my remarks to one significant aspect of this redefinition: the revaluation of work. The phrase *occupation honnête* as a synonym for (paid) labor, which we find in the article "Idleness" (OISIVETÉ [*Droit nat. & polit.*]),[9] already reveals the authors' aspirations to free work from the aristocratic contempt to which it had been subject. For the aristocratic *honnête homme*, after all, work was not an *honnête* activity.

The new work ethic was legitimated by appeals to human nature. Only through work, claimed Jaucourt in the article, could the human being realize himself. But which activities counted as work? Where did idleness begin? The criterion was clear: *usefulness to society* was the measure of the honorability of any activity: "The practice of *idleness* is contrary to the duties of man and the citizen, whose obligation in general is to be good for something, and in particular, to make himself useful to the society of which he is a member. Nothing can relieve anyone of this duty, for it is one imposed by nature."[10] The *honnête homme* realized himself as a human being through activities useful to society. When the Encyclopedists speak of concrete human beings, it is always from the perspective of their social utility. Countless descriptions of various productive activities, from the crafts to the article "Planting" (PLANTATION), make clear in what that utility consisted. That which was specifically human, the individual's exercise of reason, was always a step forward for humanity in general. The "tremendous achievements of man" (article HOMME [*Morale*]) were inextricably linked to universal human progress. Specifically human activity was always social.

Woman as Natural Being in the Physiocrats' *Ordre Naturel*

The socially useful (i.e., productive) activities of human beings, however, were defined in the *Encyclopédie* as a strictly male business. We look in vain for the female counterpart to the *honnête homme*, the *honnête femme*. The fact that this term—in contrast to the ubiquity of its male equivalent—appears, so far as I could discover, but once in the *Encyclopédie* (see later discussion) is no mere formality. The authors exclude woman's work from their archived knowledge, or rather, they suppress it in favor of another form of female productivity: fertility. The disproportion between articles on woman's social activities and her biological nature in the *Encyclopédie* is striking. A multiplicity of articles (e.g., the entries "womb, birth, breasts, wet nurse, menstruation") assemble what was known about the peculiarities of the female body, with an emphasis on childbirth and breast-feeding.

The exclusion of women's work stands in stark contrast to social reality. Léon Abensour has demonstrated that women played as great a role as men in eighteenth-century economic life.[11] This ignoring of women's

artisanal, agricultural, and intellectual labor, together with the simulta-
neous marked interest in the biological side of their humanity, reflects,
I believe, the Encyclopedists' *physiocratically oriented social theory*.
Woman's value as a human being—like man's—lay in her usefulness to
society. This usefulness, however, as the physiocratic economists understood it, lay not so much in the productivity of her labor as in her biological capacity to produce human life. As Diderot wrote in his programmatic article HOMME (*Politique*),

> There is no other true wealth than *man* and land. *Man* is worthless without
> land, and land is worthless without *man*. *Man* is valuable in numbers; the
> more numerous a society is, the more powerful it will be during times of peace,
> and the more formidable during times of war. A sovereign will attend seri-
> ously to the multiplication of his subjects. The more subjects he has, the more
> merchants, workmen and soldiers there will be.[12]

For the Physiocrats, the assurance of population growth was as important a factor as arable land. The *biological reproduction of human beings* gained new significance against the background of their population
policies and the broad demographic discussion they initiated in the eighteenth century. This aspect was intensified by the fact that contemporaries in eighteenth-century France lived with a sense of population crisis.
Although, in contrast to the preceding century, this period experienced a
thirty percent growth in the French population (from 21.5 to 29 million),
the increase went unnoticed by contemporaries. The French were still
haunted by the great mortality crises of the past, and the entire century
lived in the shadow of a myth of stagnation.[13]

This consciousness did correspond to an *objective* crisis of the household economy, one which spawned an unprecedented wave of child
neglect. The growth of child abandonment in the eighteenth century was
an eloquent expression of this widespread abuse. In 1772, at the height
of this development, seven thousand abandoned children were admitted
to the "Couche," the hospital responsible for foundlings, in Paris alone.[14]
Diderot speaks of five thousand child abandonments a year in his article
"Man" (HOMME [*Politique*]).

The Physiocrats' theories describe this state of affairs as a squandering
of wealth in the form of human labor power, and women became the
main addressees of the economists' alarm signals. Elisabeth Badinter
has shown the great ideological significance that the propagation of the
mother role held within physiocratic discourse.[15] By locating woman's

social utility in her biological particularity, the natural side of her humanity took on quite another significance than it held for the natural being man.

In the *Encyclopédie*, this shift of emphasis was expressed as a liberation of woman from the medieval-clerical constraints which had long surrounded her sex. Here we no longer encounter the pejorative connotations of femininity which still belonged as a matter of course to the knowledge assembled in the Jesuit *Dictionnaire de Trévoux*, whose entry "Woman" (FEMME) included misogynist proverbs.[16] For Enlightenment thinkers *woman's biological nature* became an object of knowledge to be grasped rationally. To a great extent, the *Encyclopédie* treats female physiology and maladies with strict medical matter-of-factness (see, e.g., the article "Woman in childbed" [FEMME EN COUCHE]).[17] This is true even in those cases which seem most open to all manner of misogynist speculation. In the article "Menstruation" (MENSTRUES [*Médecine*]),[18] the misogynist myths surrounding menstruation are labeled superstition, although even the most progressive physicians of the age possessed no plausible explanation for the phenomenon.

The desire to allow sexuality—as an economic factor—to develop optimally and in a form appropriate to bourgeois society also led to a revision in conceptions of marriage. If the aim and purpose of marriage was to produce children, as Jaucourt expressly emphasizes in the article "Marriage" (MARIAGE [*Droit nat.*]), then the appropriate conditions had to be created. It was thus necessary to prevent young people from being married off against their will, since this deprived the state (!) of "women's few, precious years of fertility."[19] Jaucourt thus argues against forced marriages and marriages contracted for social position.

By producing and raising children, the married couple fulfilled its function, and Jaucourt saw no objections to divorce once they had discharged this duty. His reasoning once more reveals clearly the close ties between emancipatory demands grounded in natural law and the anthropological definition of men and women as natural beings:

> Because the aim of the association between the male and the female is not simply to procreate, but also to perpetuate the species, this association must continue at least as long after procreation as is necessary for the nourishment and preservation of offspring, that is to say, until they are capable of taking care of themselves. This is the principal and perhaps the only reason why male and female human beings are required to continue their association longer than other animals.[20]

This attitude leads to the notion of marriage as a civil contract, as opposed to the church's understanding of marriage as a sacrament. If we recall that one of the central demands of the *Cahiers de doléances* written by women before the French Revolution was the right to divorce,[21] the emancipatory significance of the natural law concept of marriage articulated here becomes more apparent.

Finally, we should not underestimate the demographic discourse's legitimizing function for the Enlightenment's rehabilitation of sensuality in the face of clerical prudery. In his article "Celibacy" (CÉLIBAT [*Hist. anc. & mod. Morale*]),[22] Diderot had calculated the sum lost annually to the state through priestly celibacy by putting a price of 9 pounds sterling on each child not born because of the injunction against priestly marriage (following the Englishman Bernard de Mandeville). Under the entry "Sensual" (VOLUPTUEUX), he informs his gentle readers:

> Those who teach I know not what austere doctrine which would reproach us for the sensitivity of the organs bestowed upon us by nature, whose desire it was that the preservation of the species and ourselves should afford us pleasure; and for that multitude of objects that surround us and that are destined to affect that sensitivity in a hundred agreeable ways, are so many melancholics who should be locked up in an asylum.[23]

The Other Side of the Natural Order

Other consequences of the physiocratic notion of femaleness were to have a more drastic effect on women's fate within the culture, however. By directly locating women's role in social reproduction in her natural bodily functions, the Physiocrats equated woman's humanity with her creatureliness. *Her humanity consisted chiefly in her sexual destiny.* She was *le sexe*, an expression used as a synonym for *woman*.[24]

According to the testimony of the *Encyclopédie*, this notion led to a continual emphasis on the incompatibility between female nature and woman's capacity to control nature. It was not the implicit equation of human being with man which was the real disgrace but, rather, the—equally unspoken—equation of woman with sex. The unchanging female nature attributed to women served as justification for keeping them in their supposedly creaturely place. The concept of nature here does not serve as a foundation for mature independence and freedom. Rather, it demarcates the limits of proper social behavior. A woman who overstepped these boundaries incurred the wrath of nature. As an example, one need only point to the numerous tracts in which women who refused to breast-feed were confronted with horrific cautionary tales about the supposedly dire effects of milk blockages.[25]

I would like to sketch the *domesticatory function of the concept of female nature*, taking the discursive strategy of the article "Midwife" (ACCOUCHEUSE) as an example. In this text, authored by Diderot, the midwife's work is described as the devil's own. With something close to relish, he reports on the deformities (supposedly witnessed by himself) caused by the cruelties and ignorance of the midwife and announces, by means of a quotation from La Mettrie, the enlightened male public's opinion of this profession—which by the way is the only female trade to which the *Encyclopédie* devotes an article. "Women would be better off . . . if there were no midwives. The art of midwifery is inappropriate unless there are obstacles: but these women do not await the time appointed by nature; they tear the egg, & drag out the baby before the woman's pains have truly commenced."[26] As a rule, women should not require midwives; they only had to wait for nature to take its course. Any attempt to control their own nature was to court disaster. A few pages before, the entry "Childbed" (ACCOUCHEMENT) provided four pages of precise instructions for assisting childbirth. The assistant mentioned, however, is not a "midwife" (*accoucheuse*), but a "surgeon" (*chirurgien*). What is forbidden to the midwife/woman is the duty of the surgeon/man. It is his nature to intervene in nature, investigating and transforming. While female nature is constantly reminding women of the "natural" limits of creaturely existence, male nature rises ever higher above it. While male nature develops through the productive activities of practical and theoretical labors, female nature is trapped in the cycles of organic reproduction.

In future, the biological determination of female nature was to become a convincing argument for legitimating the idea of natural sex-specific character.[27] The *Encyclopédie* only hints at this conclusion: "If that same delicacy of the organs that renders *women's* imaginations more lively also renders their minds less capable of attention, one can also say that they perceive more quickly, see as well and look more cursorily."[28]

That man sometimes came to fear the monster he had created by constructing female nature was a fate he brought upon himself. The female biology conjured up by men threatened at times to slip out of their control. Medical research, whose failings were a subject of agreement among the physicians who wrote for the *Encyclopédie*, did not succeed in ban-

ishing all the unpredictabilities of female natural power. Hippocrates'
warnings about the uterus were still taken seriously in the eighteenth
century. The article "Womb" (MATRICE), which went on for pages about
the "maladies" which befell this organ, began with the Hippocratic theory
that "the smallest disturbance in this organ results in a general disorder
of the machine as a whole; one may claim with confidence that there is
scarcely an illness which affects women in which the womb does not play
some part."[29]

In the article "Marriage" (MARIAGE), (which is also a synonym for sexual
intercourse), Ménuret de Chambaud describes the natural power of female
sexuality. "Once they become carried away, they forget the laws of
modesty and propriety, seeking by any and all means to satisfy their wild
passions; they attack men shamelessly, enticing them with the most in-
decent poses and lascivious propositions."[30] He speaks here of women
who are sexually unsatisfied. To prevent them from disturbing the social
order, they must be married off as quickly as possible. The unmarried
woman does not conform to the norm and is considered either licentious
(*debauchée*) or of necessity neuropathic from sexual deprivation. "All
practitioners agree that the various symptoms of the vapors or of the
hysterical afflictions which affect young girls and widows are a result of
sexual deprivation [*privation de mariage*]."[31] The life of unmarried
women was diagnosed as an illness, and the doctors already had some
remedies in mind:

> Physicians are often obliged to marry these patients off, and the success of
> this remedy proves the correctness of their advice. . . . There are a thousand
> circumstances in which coitus legitimated by marriage is impossible, and
> religion does not permit us to imitate the fortuitous audacity of Rolfink, who
> saw no other means to cure a dangerously sick woman than to cause an ex-
> pulsion of her semen [which it was believed women also had]. Since no hus-
> band was at hand, he used an artificial object for this purpose and achieved
> a complete recovery.[32]

The Moral Sex

Woman's biological nature was not simply a physical problem of interest to physicians. Because it was intended to be channeled for the good
of society, this nature also had a genuinely social dimension. When the
social function of woman's nature was set down as a binding norm, this

raised the issue of morality in the narrower sense of the word: not simply as an anthropological definition of woman but also as the generalized social expectation of particular modes of behavior. Since woman's duties were to be restricted to the functioning of her biological nature, her morality, too, referred mainly to her sex-specific character (i.e., concretely speaking, to her sexual behavior).

In the article "Woman" (FEMME [*Morale*]), a description of the sophisticated salons, portrayed as sites of immorality, serves to distinguish specifically female morality. The social life of the *monde* is characterized in lavish detail as a corrupt one which deforms female character. The author Desmahis describes a type of woman he calls Chloë whom he locates within the aristocracy: "She bears a great name." Chloë experiments with love, which appears as her sex's sole reason for being.[33] As an archetypical representative of Paris salon culture who has chosen fashionable sociability as her life's work, she is portrayed as a woman in a world of superficial vanities who has ceased to follow her heart. Desmahis makes unmistakeably clear his disapproval of amorous intrigue as a way of life for women. The description of the course taken by Chloë's life is meant to serve as a deterrent to others. The author warns his female readers against seeking their happiness among the *monde*, which would prove to be their moral downfall. It is in this context that the term *honnête femme* appears—used exclusively, however, in the sense of "decent, chaste woman"—in contrast to aristocratic libertinage.

> Flirtatious in the extreme, she nevertheless believes herself merely coquettish. In this conviction she sits at the gaming-table; now attentive, now distracted, she answers the first man with her knee, squeezes the hand of the next, praising his laces, and at the same moment tosses a few apposite words to a third. She claims to be without prejudice because she has no principles; she assumes the title "honnête homme" because she has renounced that of *honnête femme*.[34]

His protagonist plays with her lovers according to the rules of fashionable society; her behavior is guided by pretence rather than genuine feeling: "[S]he knows how to give sensuality all the appearance of sentiment, and pleasure all the charms of sensuality. She is equally adept at hiding desires and feigning emotion, at putting on a smile and shedding a tear. Her eyes rarely betray what is in her soul; her lips almost never speak what her eyes reveal, or what is in her soul."[35] The observing philosopher concludes, "Who can define women? Everything in them speaks, but in an equivocal language. . . . Women's souls are like their beauty; it seems that they only let it be seen in order to fire the imagination!"[36] The author, however, is by no means using his imagination. Rather, he follows his morally disapproving portrait of the flirtatious woman with her opposite, a representation gleaned not from his own fantasy, but depicting in concentrated form the moral definition of woman as expressed in the Enlightenment conception of femininity.

> [H]er happiness is to know nothing of what the elegant world [*le monde*] calls *pleasures*; her glory is to live in obscurity. Confined to the duties of wife and mother, she devotes her days to the practice of unheroic virtues: occupied with running her family, she rules her husband with indulgence, her children with gentleness, and her servants with kindness. Her home is a haven of religious sentiment, filial piety, conjugal love, maternal affection, order, inner peace, sweet slumber, & health: thrifty and domestic, she keeps passions and desires at bay; no pauper presenting himself at her doorstep is ever turned away; no licentious man ever presents himself. She is respected for the reserve & dignity of her character, loved for her leniency & sensitivity & feared for her prudence & firmness. She spreads a sweet warmth, a pure light which illumines and enlivens all that surrounds her. Was it nature that placed her on the highest level, at which I find her, or was it reason that led her there?[37]

Woman is accorded a secure place here, sited in a triple sense: anthropologically as the "ruler" in the sphere of human reproduction; socially as a (bourgeois) housewife and mother; morally as a chaste person living in seclusion whose destiny (to love) manifests itself solely in the family sphere. Desmahis' rhetorical question "Who can define women?" appears to refer not to women in general, but only to women of a particular social stratum. It is the *femme du monde* who is so indefinable for him; her "unnatural" way of life distorts human nature to the point of unrecognizability. He nonetheless by no means dispenses with a concrete definition of the feminine more generally. On the contrary, his normative model of the housewife and mother is the standpoint from which not only the critique of the nonbourgeois woman is formulated, but also from which the nature of woman within the Encyclopedist's anthropological system is defined.

While the article "Man" (HOMME [*Morale*]) addresses Man's relationship to nature as a whole, the article "Woman" (FEMME [*Morale*]) concentrates solely on woman's relationship to her own (i.e., sexual) nature. As a result, woman, in contrast to man, is not regarded from the standpoint of intellectual perfectability but chiefly from the standpoint of moral improvement, with an emphasis on her sexual morals.

Whereas LeRoy, as we have seen, demonstrated man's superiority to animals by pointing to his great scientific achievements in the article "Man" (HOMME [*Morale*]), Desmahis makes woman's virtuousness the determining factor of her humanity. Woman's intellectual capacity, her actual or potential role in human knowledge or scientific progress is no longer part of the discussion. The devoted wife and mother, the paradigm of female happiness, is defined by moral qualities such as complaisance, gentleness, forbearance, and sensitivity.

The often quite extensive articles on child-rearing, on school curricula, and on the institutionalization of education nowhere address girls or women.[38] Only in the odd phrase is their intellectual improvement mentioned at all.[39] The sole goal of exercising their intellect is to educate their *moral* judgment. For Barthez the function of women's learning is to "weaken their sinful tendencies."[40] Desmahis also hands women a bit of unambiguous advice for the use of their reason: "There is a woman whose wit makes her loved rather than feared. . . ."[41] For him, the deficiencies of girls' education are, above all, a moral danger: "It is astonishing that such uncultivated souls could bring forth so many virtues, and that more vice does not sprout there."[42] The *Dictionnaire raisonné* pays no heed to Poulain de la Barre and his followers. Compared to discussions up to that time, the authors of the *Encyclopédie*, that very work which prided itself on assembling the knowledge of its age, pay little tribute to the learned woman. In the article "Woman" (FEMME [*Anthropologie*]), Barthez may express his wonderment at the large number of illustrious women, but he only mentions one, Anna Maria Schurmann, whom contemporaries regarded as a "paradigm of female learning."[43] His passage cannot be viewed as an homage to this unusual woman either; the euphoria of feminist texts in the rationalist tradition has given way to a more skeptical evaluation. Mallet considers Schurmann's argument "that scholarly studies enlighten and provide a wisdom one cannot buy with the perilous aid of experience" a mere excuse, insisting that "it is doubtful whether this premature caution does not cost a bit of innocence."[44]

By focusing above all on woman's social role as mother, the *Encyclopédie* can no longer formulate an equality between men and women in the sense of identical (intellectual) abilities. In contrast to the rationalist feminists' position, which abstracted from social conditions, the discourse on woman in the *Encyclopédie* is grounded in Enlightenment thinkers' notion of society.

The *Encyclopédie* reflects the conflict between bourgeois concepts of society and the emancipatory drive for education. The Encyclopedists' socioeconomic ideas, which culminate in numerous articles in calls for stable family structures and population growth, left their mark on the articles on women. The demands for education made in passing throughout the *Encyclopédie* are not followed up either by references to existing approaches or concrete suggestions for reform. The bourgeois way of life no longer permitted equality in the use of reason.

It is against this background, I believe, that we must evaluate Desmahis' article "Woman" (FEMME [*Morale*]). The function of this text, which at first glance seems more anecdotal than analytical, is to make women's exclusion from the public sphere appear reasonable. The author's warnings against fashionable sociability are more than the simple expression of a general rejection of the way of life of the Ancien Régime's parasitic upper crust which we find in a number of articles throughout the *Encyclopédie*. While elsewhere condemnations of aristocratic idleness culminate in demands for new, more useful forms of sociability than those prevailing in the *monde*,[45] Desmahis' demonization of the lady of fashion serves to justify woman's complete exclusion from social communication. Bourgeois woman's virtue was not to be expressed in the development of new forms of social intercourse within the framework of an enlightened counterpublic, as articulated for example by Saint-Lambert in the article (HONNÊTE). "Her glory" was, rather, "to live in obscurity."

It was precisely here, though, that Desmahis touched the weak point of Enlightenment strategies of legitimation. When he speaks of the virtuous woman as one living "in obscurity," "enclosed" within the sphere of her domestic duties, he reveals the conflict just described—that the process of excluding women from public life also means their exclusion from intellectual exchange, all the more so when one considers that a good portion of intellectual communication—also and particularly among the Encyclopedists—took place in salons. This explains the eloquent silence hanging over the learned woman in the *Encyclopédie*.

Women's capacity for rational thought, however, had not yet been excluded altogether. It remained an empty space, which was filled in the 1770s by two theoretical texts. While the *Encyclopédie* avoided the question of female learning, both Antoine Léonard Thomas and Pierre Roussel were to devote much attention to the subject.

3

The Sensualist Turning Point

The writings of Thomas and Roussel may be regarded as occupying representative positions in the late-Enlightenment *querelle des femmes*. The many reviews of Thomas' *Essai sur les femmes* (Essay on Women) in contemporary journals, and the fact that it inspired Diderot's own essay *Sur les femmes*, point to the work's broad reception. Roussel's *Système physique et moral de la femme* (Systematic Overview of Woman as Physical and Moral Being) went through numerous editions into the second half of the nineteenth century.[1]

Thomas' *Essai* cannot, however, be regarded as an original text. It is, rather, an agreeable summary of the *querelle des femmes* since the middle of the eighteenth century. The passages concerned with moral-philosophical considerations, in particular, are highly indebted, without explicit acknowledgment, to the ideas of Rousseau, or to the reception of his works, particularly *La Nouvelle Héloïse*. This kind of text seems to me just the place to learn which aspects of the mid-century *querelle* had gained intellectual influence. In a later chapter on Rousseau I will examine those finer points of Rousseau's positions that were lost in the "popular" reception of his works.

The historian Thomas and the physician Roussel agreed that the answer to the question of woman's intellectual capacity depended on her biological nature. According to Thomas, "We must see . . . to what degree . . . the natural weakness of their [women's] organs permits the intense and lasting attention required to sustain a long continuous train of thought."[2] Roussel believed that reflections on women's "moral" nature could only proceed on the basis of physiological knowledge. "Having considered woman from the physical standpoint, I then examined her from the intellectual standpoint. In so doing, I have doubtless restored medicine to its rights. I have always been persuaded that it is only in this discipline that the foundations of good morals lie. . . ."[3] The shift of the *querelle des femmes* to the plane of sensory physiology made possible the strict separation of femininity and masculinity in *all* aspects of life. For Poulain de la Barre and his followers, woman's biological nature had played only an insignificant role in regard to her intellectual capabilities, because, in the Cartesian tradition, they gave precedence to reason, which they conceived of as genderless. Thomas and Roussel, in contrast, proceeded from woman's physiological constitution in order to determine her intellectual capacity.

This reversal of perspective must be viewed against the background of a changed epistemological position within philosophy which also resulted in radical changes within medicine, particularly neurology.[4] The transition from rationalism to sensualism brought with it a shift of emphasis in notions of the origin and uniqueness of human knowledge. Surely, Descartes had taken account of both sides of knowledge—perception and cognition. One need only point to his extensive discussion of sensory physiology in the *Traité de l'homme* (Treatise on Man).[5] But the certainty of knowledge could only come from reason, which as *res cogitans* was in principle independent of the sensory impressions of *res extensa*. During the eighteenth century this autonomy of reason remained fundamentally unchallenged. To that extent Poulain's dictum of incorporeal, and thus gender-neutral, intellect could still claim validity.

Nevertheless, it cannot be overlooked that ever since Locke's *Essay Concerning Human Understanding* and more particularly Condillac's *Essai sur l'origine des connaissances humaines* (Essay on the Origin of Human Knowledge), the concepts processed by reason, and to some extent also the connection of these concepts, were attributed primarily to sensory perception or experience.[6] In this way, knowledge was made dependent on the human physiological constitution. Questions surrounding the nature of the sensory organs and nerves attained greater significance than had been the case for Descartes and his adherents. In addition, the knowing subject no longer attained certainty through direct evidence but rather through self-perception. Human beings observed the operations of their own reason, which themselves had become an empirical object.[7]

All of this had become the object of an anthropology that placed the human being's natural condition at its center. Here human nature was not, as it had been for Descartes, for example, that which was original and essential but rather, quite literally, the physical-material condition of the human being. Surmounting, at least partially, the traditional dualism of nature and intellect, a theory of the intellectual capacities of the sexes could no longer ignore the physical differences between men and women which Poulain had still managed to exclude. This was to have fateful consequences for the learned woman. I would like to treat these two works beginning from this standpoint.

Roussel, who provided a precise description of the female organism according to the medical knowledge of his day, points to the "immediate effects, which appear to stem from the organization of woman's sensitive body parts."[8] The superior softness and mobility of women's bodily organs resulted in a greater sensitivity of the nerves and thus in quicker and more subtle sensory perceptions. This intensity and simultaneity of the most varied perceptions, however, made women incapable of abstraction: "The difficulty of shedding the tyranny of her sensations constantly binds her to the immediate causes which call them [the sensations] forth, preventing her from rising to those heights which would afford her a view of the whole."[9] Woman, thus, has more sensitive perceptions than man, but it is precisely this superiority which hinders her from grasping broader connections, because she is dominated by immediate sensory impressions. On the way to more complex concepts, woman finds herself at a standstill. Since, under empirical conditions, only this inductive method leads to universal knowledge, the fate of the learned woman is sealed.

We find the same assessment in Thomas, to whose *tableau énergique & élégant* Roussel incidentally refers. Thomas still shows the influence of Poulain when he complains that in previous "defenses of women" "reasoning has everywhere been replaced by authority, even when speaking of women; but on this matter, as on many others, twenty quotations are not worth a single argument!"[10] His line of argument, however, unlike Poulain's, does not proceed from a presumption of fundamental intellectual equality but from a comparison of bodily organs. "It seems that, in order to decide, once and for all, the great point of pride and rivalry between the two sexes, we must examine the strength or weakness of the bodily organs."[11] This sensualist position shifts the problem of "rivalry" between the sexes from the rational-intellectual to the sensory-physiological plane, thus rendering physical constitution a decisive determinant of intellectual capacity.

Thomas distinguishes four different operations of reason: the "philosophical spirit, which reflects" (*esprit philosophique qui médite*), "memory, which associates" (*esprit de mémoire qui rassemble*), "imagination, which creates" (*esprit d'imagination qui crée*), and the "political or moral spirit, which governs" (*esprit politique ou moral qui gouverne*).[12] Not surprisingly, he appeals to Descartes, who, to his mind, wrongly attributed the philosophical spirit to women (perhaps he means Poulain here?). Thomas does not consider woman capable of philosophical reflection because her mind, dominated by a multiplicity of impressions, is too inclined to jump back and forth between objects instead of focusing on one at a time in order to reach more profound insights. "It [woman's intellect] contains more wit than effort. What it cannot grasp at once, it either does not see, or rejects, or despairs at ever seeing. It would thus be scarcely surprising if it were lacking in that stubborn slowness which alone seeks and discovers great truths."[13] Woman may possess a quick understanding, but she lacks the thoroughness and the will to apply herself that are necessary to achieve true knowledge. Thomas attributes this deficiency to the "natural weakness of her organs, from which her beauty arises . . . the restlessness of her character, stemming from her imagination . . . the number and variety of her sensations, which constitute part of her charm."[14] The same reasons contradict the assumption that men and women share a "spirit of order and of memory which classifies facts and ideas in order to recover them when needed."[15] In an analogy to biological differences, Thomas claims, "We know that there exist intellectual abilities which are mutually exclusive. One cannot use the same hand to cut a diamond and to drive a gallery [in the mines]."[16] Thomas has thus already answered his final, purely rhetorical question of whether women's education, or women's nature, is responsible for the dearth of famous women compared to men "in favor" of women's nature.

Roussel advances further physiological arguments for woman's limited intellectual capacity. The assumed sensitivity of the entire female organism can withstand no extraordinary strain. For this reason, he warns against excessive physical effort. Continuous studies, however, are even more harmful than physical labor. Even in men, the "strong exertion of the intellectual powers" would lead to an unhealthy concentration of bodily fluids in the brain. The result was the "vapors" (*vapeurs*), a term for supposed hysteria, that is, for a whole range of nondiagnosable, chiefly psychosomatic illnesses. Another physician, Raulin, had already pointed to women's greater disposition to "vaporous afflictions" (*affections vapeureuses*) in 1758.[17] The conclusions Roussel draws go beyond his colleague's. "Her delicate organs will feel more keenly the unavoidable ill effects that serious study brings with it!"[18] For this reason, nature had equipped women with healthy instincts which shepherded them safely past the dangerous abysses of scholarship. For Roussel, the theory of usurpation with which Poulain and his followers had explained female ignorance was nothing but the flattery of a few unprincipled men. "Those men who seek to flatter women maintain . . . that we bar the door to the sciences before them, in order to secure this privilege exclusively for ourselves. The truth is that they do not care a whit for them [the sciences], and rightfully so. One wants to praise them for the intellect they might have, as if there were not enough to commend in the intellect they do have."[19] Henceforth, woman could only persist in trying to cross the threshhold of the sciences at the expense of losing her normatively defined, gender-specific identity. Femininity and learning had become two incompatible quantities. Roussel describes the consequences of scholarly endeavor in a truly deterrent manner: "A person who devotes herself deeply exists only in the head; she scarcely appears to breathe. The body, deprived of regenerating juices . . . languishes, fades and, at length, dwindles like a tender shrub planted in arid soil, whose branches have been parched by the torrid sun."[20] In contrast to their limited capacity for rational reflection, Thomas accords women great powers of imagination because of their "mobile senses, [which] skim all objects, retaining their image. . . . The real world is not enough for them; they delight in creating an imaginary one, which they inhabit and embellish."[21] This capacity for fantasy, which is always mentioned primarily as a disposition toward superstition, exercised the minds of the time. Women react to outside influences like sensitive seismographs and were thus more receptive to sensory impressions—but also more susceptible to sensory illusions. This premise led to the presumption of great female powers of imagination that—in contrast to male imagination, which was ruled and controlled by reason—continually threatened to slip into irrationality and superstition. "Ghosts, enchantments, wonders, all that is outside the ordinary laws of nature, are their work and their delight. Their souls are elated and their minds ever closer to enthusiasm."[22] The supposed power of this greater capacity for imagination, and the supposed feebleness of the reduced capacity for thought, are attributed in both cases to woman's particular physical constitution.

It would nevertheless be hasty to attribute to Roussel and Thomas the conception that reason itself took on a specifically female character. Caution is necessary here: women are not being denied in principle the capacity for reason, which is still conceived as gender neutral. Roussel and Thomas do, however, deny them the necessary preconditions for developing this reason as men do. The discovery that the sensory organs exert an influence over human knowledge is used to shape the argument that women are incapable of certain cognitive operations. The same conditions that, according to Locke, make human knowledge possible in the first place, are now seen as having the opposite effect. In women, the very sensory perceptions that provide men with the materials for their cognitive labors are turned into obstacles to certain cognitive functions. The female sex may have quicker and more precise perceptions, but women are incapable of abstraction and thus of cognitive accomplishments comparable to men's.

The dismantling of women's capacity for thought and creativity on the grounds of their physical constitution went hand in hand with a new definition and valorization of femininity, derived from precisely this biological determination: the ability to bear children as a genuinely feminine corporeality. As the *Encyclopédie* already hinted, there was no discourse on women in the late Enlightenment which did not mention this sex-specific bodily function at least implicitly. In the next chapter I take a closer look at this phenomenon.

4

The Sexualization of Female Existence

The transition to a sensualist or naturalist anthropology of woman was no mere shift of epistemological or scientific paradigms. From the very beginning, the distribution of sensory and cognitive capacities between the sexes had a social character. It was argued that woman, because of her physical constitution, possessed more sensitivity and less rationality than man and was thus better able to fulfill a particular social function. This fusion of sociability and nature becomes particularly apparent in the discourse on female sexuality. For the sensualist theoreticians, the specificity of female nature reveals itself nowhere more clearly than in those bodily functions directly dependent on sex.

Medical Discourse

The proliferation of literature dealing with the female body and more particularly with women's sexuality is striking. This phenomenon can be observed both in the literary and medical fields. The multitude of popular medical treatises in particular testify to the dominant consciousness of the Enlightenment.[1] Michel Delon has described the effort to recognize and express the specificity of the female organism as opposed to the male as a characteristic of medical discourse. This dissociation (gradually) came to replace the ancient theory regarding the female body as derivative of the male, a view which retained its validity into the eighteenth century. "In relation to man, woman is regarded either as a lack, an excess or, in a more developed theory, as an inversion."[2] The male body and its functions—so far as they were known—represented the norm, and the definition of the female body consisted in a compilation of deviations from this norm. The universal ignorance surrounding the female reproductive organs strengthened the tendency to define woman's entire organism as a mere variation on the male. Woman was viewed as a "deficient man" (*homme manqué*). The lack of a specific medical terminology for describing the female body is typical.[3] In addition, Enlightenment physicians also referred to Galen, who, proceeding from the Aristotelian thesis of the *homme manqué*, described the female genitals as internalized and only partially developed forms of the male organs. This view led Buffon to argue that scientists should devote themselves more to finding the homologies between the male and female organisms: "[I]n reflecting upon the structure of the generative parts of each sex of the human species, one finds so many resemblances and such a singular conformity that one might be led to believe that those parts which appear so different to us on the outside are, in truth, the same organs."[4] In the article FEMME (*Anthropologie*) in the *Encyclopédie* Barthez, citing Daubenton, similarly reduces the biological differences between men and women:

> M. Daubenton . . . having noticed the greatest analogy between the two sexes in the secretion and emission of semen, believes that the only difference one can find in the size & position of certain parts depends solely upon the womb which is additionally present in women, & that this organ, were men to possess it, would make their reproductive organs absolutely identical to those of women.[5]

These physiological theories admitted of no extensive sex-specific distinctions. Roussel, who developed the first systematic female physiology in 1779, bemoaned this state of affairs:

> If philosophers on the one hand have observed the moral side well, physicians, on the other, have described the physical well, at least as far as is possible. The latter would have done well, however, to pay greater attention to woman's constitution in general, & and not simply to regard her as a being completely identical to man, except for those particular functions that characterize her sex.[6]

In contrast to contemporary medical literature, Roussel emphasized men's and women's *different* functions in reproduction, viewing these biological differences as a universal principle encompassing *all* of life:

> There are authors who believed they had found much resemblance between the genital parts of women and men. Rest assured that these authors have been misled by false or superficial reports. The different functions of man and woman in the important task of procreation alone suffice to remove any idea of similarity between the organs with which each participates.[7]

For him, woman is not an *homme manqué*. Instead, her membership in the female sex shapes her entire physical and psychic constitution, which differs in every respect from man's. Roussel does not stop at the feminization of the female body. The entire female organism is, in his view, designed to perform a function assigned to woman by nature, one which consists not merely in childbearing but also extends to her social role. It is the physician's task to explore this function systematically. Henceforth femaleness was no longer an (anatomical) attribute but a principle within the anthropological system as a whole. Each part of the female organism was a mark of woman's destiny. In this Roussel departs decisively from materialistic theories (e.g., La Mettrie's and Helvétius'), which regarded the intellectual (and also physical) differences between human beings as the result of outside influences and education. For him, the differences between man and woman were both innate (*innées*) and determinant of their character. "It is probable, then, that the arrangement of those parts which compose woman's body is determined by nature herself, and that it serves as the *foundation* [emphasis added] of the physical and moral character which distinguishes her [from man]."[8] Roussel assumes an eternal feminine and an eternal masculine principle, which are expressed in the physical nature of human beings. As I demonstrated in the previous chapter, he (re)constructed female sex-specific character largely through pure analogies to women's physique, justifying his approach with the assertion that woman's constitution was finalistic, that is, essentially grounded in her capacity for reproduction.

Roussel's treatise is typical of the biological-medical dimension of the paradigmatic shift. In it we see the process, typical for the eighteenth century, of the complete sex-specific determination of the female individual. Scientific discourse was the precondition for the later view of female human beings primarily as sexual beings. Diderot's literary representations provide an excellent illustration of this phenomenon.

Literary Discourse

Sur les femmes

This little text[9] was written in response to Antoine-Léonard Thomas'
Essai sur les femmes, which was discussed earlier. Diderot criticizes
the neutral distance to his subject which Thomas adopted as an author.
He calls for a discourse that proceeds from the female human being's
sexual destiny. According to him, the topic of women can only be treated
in the context of their sexuality. Thus he traces all manifestations
of woman's life back to her sexual organs. The relationship between
femaleness and irrational feeling, still vague in Thomas' work, reveals
itself in Diderot's review as a clinical diagnosis: hysteria. The anoma-
lies of female imagination—which Diderot treats at some length as cases
of mass hysteria, superstition, religious fanaticism, prophecy, and self-
destruction—are for him not exceptions but central features of female
sexuality.

In contrast to the norm—male sexuality—Diderot views female sexuality as oscillating between the poles of frigidity and excess. Measuring
it against controlled virile regularity, he finds female desire wanting.
"Less in control of their senses than we are, the rewards are also less
prompt and less sure for them."[10] The lack of control over their own sensuality was also the cause of the excessive feelings that erupted in bouts
of hysteria: "The woman dominated by hysteria feels I know not what
infernal or celestial emotions. At times she makes me shiver. I have seen
and heard in her the raging of the ferocious beast which is a part of her."[11]
This lack of self-control is in the very nature of the female sexual organs.
When he speaks of them, Diderot's discourse evokes danger: "Woman
carries within herself an organ subject to terrible spasms, ruling her and
exciting in her imagination phantasms of all sorts. . . . It is from the organ
peculiar to her sex that all kinds of extraordinary ideas emerge."[12]
Woman's dependence on her sexuality prevents her advancement to a
higher stage of civilization. She remains mired in humanity's original
savage state, ever threatening to sully man's cultural achievements with
an uncontrolled outbreak of her powerful natural sexuality: "Outwardly
they are more civilized than we are, but inwardly they have remained
true savages, at the very least complete Machiavellians."[13] Woman is not
receptive to humanity's moral values: "[L]acking in reflection and principles, nothing penetrates to a certain depth of conviction in women's
minds . . . the ideas of justice, virtue, vice, kindness, maliciousness swim

on the surface of their souls."[14] While Thomas had excluded the female sex from the public sphere because of particular deficiencies, Diderot now relegates woman to the realm of the mysterious, far removed from reality: "The symbol of women in general is that of the Apocalypse, on which is written: MYSTERY."[15]

Elisabeth de Fontenay interprets Diderot's representation of woman as the emancipatory counterpart to aristocratic, ecclesiastical, and scientific models of femininity. She attributes to the essay *Sur les femmes* a double taboo-breaking function. On the one hand, female sexuality is no longer excluded from discussions of woman and, on the other, woman is no longer defined as an *homme manqué* but rather as a being in her own right. She considers Diderot's rejection of a "neutral" discourse evidence that, in his reflections on woman, he was not setting himself up as an ultimate authority but rather bringing his own sexuality into his reflections. Instead of raising masculinity to a universal principle by neutralizing it, he describes it as desire:

> Diderot writes as a lover, not as a subject of knowledge, a strategist of seduction or a representative of divine judgment. . . . It is thus that we should interpret his constant recourse to the masculine first person plural: far from setting himself up as the norm from which women deviate, he emphasizes the involvement of male desire in his discourse on woman.[16]

According to this interpretation, Diderot explodes the symmetrical order of the sexes through the functions of the uterus which were peculiar to women, and which existing systems could no longer accommodate. The total conditioning of female existence by the sexual organs no longer allowed for a symmetry of the sexes and, with it, for the Cartesian image of humanity. From then on, both the sexlessness of cognition and the universality of the *res cogitans* itself were called into question:

> The uterus allows Diderot to develop his anti-Cartesian strategy, in that its bursts of rage and cunning pretences threaten the prerogative of another experience, the experience, at certain points, of the unifying thinking substance, and of the uniqueness of the subject. The pantomime of hysteria unhinges clear and distinct ideas, confuses obvious fact and scoffs at the truth: feminine peculiarity dismisses the universal masculine.[17]

Michèle Duchet makes a similar argument. She relativizes the taboo-breaking function that Fontenay claims for the essay, rightly pointing out that references to female sexuality had become commonplace in the sci-

entific and philosophical discourse of the second half of the eighteenth
century. But she also emphasizes the significance of this essay as an
attempt on Diderot's part to set himself off from Cartesianism. "Diderot's
true boldness does not lie in his theory of the female body. It lies wholly
in the connection he establishes between the physical, the moral and the
production of ideas in beings thus abandoned to the whims of an organ
that determines their behavior in advance and unbalances their conduct."[18]
Although Fontenay and Duchet are correct in their assertion that
Diderot's discourse would be unthinkable without the shift of epistemological paradigm (as I have shown), it is doubtful whether the rejection of a rationalist image of woman signified an overthrow of the
masculine hierarchically structured thought order itself. The discussion
of female sexuality, as we find it in Diderot's writings, by no means
occurs independently of norm-producing gender-neutral rationality but
rather continues to be oriented toward this norm. Not the universality
of reason is called into question, but at most its autonomy. Diderot does
in fact establish a connection between "the physical, the moral and the
production of ideas," as Duchet remarks. Nevertheless, we need to be
more precise about the respective functions of this sensualist epistemology for man and woman. The fact that in *Sur les femmes* Diderot
names the uterus as the bodily organ most important for constituting
woman's capacity for sentiment and knowledge is surely not irrelevant.
In contrast to his *Eléments de physiologie* (Elements of Physiology) and
Lettres sur les aveugles (Letters on the Blind), which are decisive for
his revision of the rationalist image of humanity, and in which he formulates the foundations for the association between knowing and feeling, in *Sur les femmes* Diderot reduces the unity of woman's body and
mind to the relationship between sex and mind—a reduction that Duchet
and Fontenay overlook. The corporeality of the female capacity for
knowledge is dominated by woman's sex-specific bodily organs. This
difference leads to a qualitative displacement. While sensations con-
tribute to the development of man's cognitive (and moral) capacity, they
tend to limit or misguide this development in woman. As a result, for
woman sensory experience and rational knowledge are mutually exclusive rather than mutually reinforcing or complementary. Fontenay's
assumption that Diderot uses the intensity of female sensation to call
into question one-dimensional (male) logic overlooks that this ques-
tioning is expressed as fear rather than opportunity. He fears that the
relics of medieval superstition will destroy the enlightened view of the

world. Female sexuality is not the paradigm for overcoming Cartesian "evidentism and apriorism." On the contrary, it is the root of ignorance, superstition, and religious fanaticism, that is, of all those phenomena that the Enlightenment opposed.

It seems to me characteristic that Diderot does not adopt the method used by the physician Raulin here. Raulin no longer sought the origins of the "vapors" solely in the uterus but incorporated the entire human—male and female—organism into his diagnosis.[19] Diderot perpetuates the myth of hidden powers at work in the female body, thus creating a site for the *mystère* banished from enlightened society. Within woman's body, those forces continued to operate that were beyond the laws of the male-dominated world. Woman thus became the favorite object of nonrational knowledge, that is, of (male) imagination. For Diderot, woman was thus both the realm that escaped rational knowledge and the place where rationalists were ordered not to use their own reason. It was for this reason that he argued against Thomas' "scientific" discourse on female nature.

Diderot's relegation of woman to the realm of *mystère* did indeed facilitate the creation of rich fantasies around woman while simultaneously abstracting from real women. It is no accident that he hotly criticized the "impartial" style of Thomas' treatise. Woman's unpredictability and natural power did not allow for matter-of-fact discourse. "In writing of women, one must dip one's pen in the rainbow and scatter the dust of butterfly wings across the page; like the pilgrim's little dog, pearls must fall with each shake of one's paw. Not a one falls from M. Thomas'."[20] Diderot himself fulfilled this demand—not only in his review of Thomas, but also in his own fictions. In his novel *La Religieuse* (The Nun), he gave the "mystery" of woman form.

La Religieuse

This novel is usually considered significant because of Diderot's blunt and realistic portrayal of convent life. His indictment of the life-denying and ultimately inhumane practices of the clergy and his appeal for the right to self-determination of a woman held in a state of tutelage are formulated with a clarity that might have put him behind bars had the book been published during his lifetime.[21] It is not my intention here to deny *La Religieuse* its status as an emancipatory novel.[22] Rather, I would like to show that it has another theme as well: the female body and female sexuality.

This theme seems at first glance to be organically woven into the tale the novel tells. Suzanne Simonin's banishment behind convent walls implies the depiction of the suppression of her sensuality and the portrayal of prudish clerical morality. It soon becomes apparent, though, that there is a second text hidden behind this one. The representation of cloistered women's suppressed sexuality is more than merely an enlightened critique of clerical celibacy, conveying at the same time male fantasies of female sexuality. The world Diderot shows the reader via his protagonist is one populated and ruled exclusively by women. Once Suzanne Simonin enters the convent, or at least once she has been admitted to holy orders, all of the characters—with the exception of the father-confessor and the lawyer—are nuns. This world is, at the same time, a medieval one, in the Enlightenment—and thus pejorative—sense. Not reason, but a ritualized belief in dogmas, determines the actions of individuals. Both elements, the world of women and the medieval world of the convent, are fused in the text to form an apparently organic whole.

Diderot conceives of the convent world—one shaped by unnatural constraints—as a sort of experimental situation. Human, in this case female, nature is placed in surroundings where human beings' supposedly innate sociability cannot develop. The results are terrible. Gentle creatures become brutal, sadistic tormentors and—lesbians. Diderot equates the two, portraying both the Mother Superior's tortures and her sexual practices as the misdirected expression of repressed drives. The boundaries between the nuns' homosexual activities and their maltreatment of Suzanne are fluid. This becomes particularly clear in the vision the Mother Superior has at the moment when her passion reaches its peak. The image of the tormented Suzanne arouses her sexual desires:

> "Drowning those eyes in tears!" And she kissed them. "Drawing groans and wailing from that mouth!" She kissed that too. "Condemning that charming, serene face to be constantly clouded by sadness!" She kissed it. "Making the roses of those cheeks wither!" She stroked them with her hand and kissed them. "Robbing that head of its beauty! tearing out that hair! loading that brow with sorrow!" She kissed my head, brow, hair. "Fancy daring to put a rope round that neck and tearing those shoulders with sharp points!" She pushed aside my collar and coif, opened the top of my dress. . . .[23]

The medieval tortures to which the Mother Superior subjects Suzanne are the complementary inversion of her amorous practices. The ultimate motive for punishing the novice is not that she resisted the order's rules but that she rebuffed the advances of the Mother Superior, who, as another nun remarked, "is capable of passing from the greatest tenderness to ferocity."[24]

The novel's anticlerical message is conveyed through forbidding images of perverted female nature. These images conjure up a "monster" woman. Although the Mother Superior is a monster created by inhumane circumstances, Diderot implies that female nature itself harbors certain perverse tendencies, which are given free reign to develop in the novel. What is more, the fear of women at the mercy of their drives—as articulated in *Sur les femmes*—guides the story here. The plot gains its tension from the expectation of the Mother Superior's continuing cruelties.

The novel evokes the image of a female nature harboring immeasurable destructive powers which are unleashed under certain conditions. Left to her own devices, woman is incapable of mastering these inherent powers. They become the undoing of the Mother Superior, for example. Her attempt to fight her own sinful inclinations ends in insanity and, finally, in death. Diderot contrasts her to the father-confessor Morel. He has recognized that the clerical estate is contrary to human nature, but he sublimates his unsatisfied drives through rational insight. While the Mother Superior destroys herself, and Suzanne continually risks her life by revolting against convent existence, their male counterpart chooses the path of the "practicable," resigning himself to his fate: "How dreadful is the condition of a nun or a priest who has no vocation! Yet it is ours and we cannot change it. We have been loaded with heavy chains which we are condemned to try ceaselessly to shake off, with no hope of breaking them; so dear sister, let us try to drag them after us."[25] Because woman is not in a position to direct her drives rationally, she is more susceptible than man to superstition, which Diderot, the man of the Enlightenment, considers the very epitome of irrationality. The fanaticism with which the nuns, especially the Mother Superior, submit to convent regulations is an eloquent example. Diderot takes up a common motif in Enlightenment literature, that of the female soul enslaved by religious superstition, and uses it against female nature in general. In *Sur les femmes* he had already described in theoretical terms what he was later to give literary shape in the Mother Superior:

> The nun in her cell feels herself lifted into the air, her soul sinks into the bosom of the divinity. Her essence unites with the divine essence; she swoons; she dwindles, her breast rises and falls at a rapid rate, the companions who sur-

round her cut the laces of the garment which constricts her. Night comes. She hears heavenly choirs; her own voice joins the concert. Then she returns to earth, speaking of ineffable joys, they listen to her, she is convinced, she is persuasive.[26]

The reliogiosity into which the Mother Superior throws herself in order to "master" her unhappy passion for Suzanne takes the form of mortification of the flesh and madness:

[S]he fasted three days a week, she scourged herself, she heard offices in the lowest stall. We had to pass her door on the way to the church, and there we saw her lying prostrate with her face to the ground, and she only rose when everybody had gone. At night she went down in her nightgown, barefoot, and if Sainte-Thérèse or I met her by chance she turned away and pressed her face against the wall. One day I emerged from my cell and found her flat on the ground with her arms extended and face to the floor, and she said: "Come on, come on and trample me underfoot. I don't deserve any other treatment."[27]

Diderot characterizes both her religious mania and her homosexual inclinations as sicknesses. "Sickness" evokes the possibility of recovery, and thus "health." Normality is only conceivable as the negation of the circumstances portrayed. Even if it is never explicitly represented, it is a constant theme. In his plea for her release, M. Manouri, Suzanne's lawyer and champion condemns conditions in the convent. He justifies this condemnation by citing the immorality that was the inevitable result of life behind convent walls:

Does God, who made man sociable, approve of his hiding himself away? Can God, who made man so inconstant and frail, authorize such rash vows? Can these vows, which run counter to our natural inclinations, ever be properly observed except by a few abnormal creatures in whom the seeds of passion are dried up, and whom we should rightly classify as freaks of nature if the state of our knowledge allowed us to understand the internal structure of man as well as we understand his external appearance? Do all these lugubrious ceremonies played out at the taking of the habit or the profession, when a man or woman is set apart for the monastic life and for woe, suspend the animal functions?[28]

The "animal functions" in question are Diderot's constant point of departure, expressing his underlying belief that our biological nature largely determines the path human beings take in life. All "lapses" along this preordained path lead to abnormality and, finally, to madness. But he leaves no doubt of what he means by women's animal functions. Manouri's (rhetorical) question provides illumination: "What need has the Bridegroom of so many foolish virgins?"[29] Virginity is directly related to the nuns' delusions. The upshot is that women who do not live according to their biological destiny are condemned to end like the hapless Mother Superior—as "monsters."

Supplément au voyage de Bougainville

Twelve years later Diderot fashioned a universe in which human beings' "animal functions" were given free reign to develop: Tahiti, the setting of his story *Supplément au voyage de Bougainville* (Supplement to Bougainville's Voyage)[30] and, like the convent, a laboratory for testing human nature. While the convent milieu may be understood as an experiment in which the human subject is studied in an artificial environment in order to gain insights into her true nature, the choice of the island location in the *Supplément* corresponds to another experimental situation, one based on the conviction that human nature can only develop fully in "natural" surroundings. While in *La Religieuse* female nature is normatively defined as a negative, focusing primarily on the "perversions" of female nature in an unnatural environment, in the *Supplément* human nature is observed in its original, that is, uncivilized state.[31] The islanders' communal life appears to be free from all social and moral constraints; the Tahitians live in harmony with each other and nature, without social hierarchy or private property.

At the story's center is a description of the sex life of the Tahitians. The conversation between the ship's chaplain and the native Ourou, in which the priest's moral attitudes are confronted with the islanders' natural sexuality, provides the narrative framework. K.- H. Kohl has convincingly shown that the story's initial claim that Tahitian society knew no artificial constraints and that the sexes enjoyed total permissiveness in their relations with each other is relativized in the course of the narrative by discussions of the sanctions imposed on particular sexual practices.[32] Thus sexual intercourse was forbidden to menstruating women, as well as to men and women no longer capable of procreation. In contrast to the ship's chaplain, however, Ourou justifies these prohibitions not with moral proscriptions, but rather with human nature itself. Human beings, like all other creatures, are subject to the eternal natural law of procreation. Biological reproduction is described as the highest principle guiding island life. To try to prevent the *actions physiques* arising from this principle with moral (i.e., nonphysical) norms was as senseless as to "abuse" them. On Tahiti the same argument is used to justify both restrictions and permissiveness: the purpose of sexuality is procreation. Since procreation was an economic necessity for Diderot, sexuality was as well.[33]

We should not, however, view Diderot's island utopia *solely* from the standpoint of his convictions on population policy. The scientific problem of biological reproduction is more important here. Since the publication of Buffon's *Histoire naturelle,* at the latest, reproduction had been adopted as a criterion for distinguishing the different species. In this context, sexuality also gained particular significance for anthropology. On the (Enlightenment) premise that physical nature provided the foundations for the development and civilization of human beings, and that it too was subject to continual development, human sexuality could serve as *the* barometer of civilizing development. Buffon, for example, takes the supposedly relatively underdeveloped sexuality of the American "savages" as proof of their social backwardness.[34] Diderot's approach is similar, but he proceeds from a different hypothesis: Assuming that the (savage) islanders have a highly developed sexuality, he considers their social development superior to that of the European nations, in which sexuality was not unleashed as a (re)productive force.

There are, however, cracks in Diderot's model of a world in which (male and female) sexuality could unfold free of normative moral constraints while preserving the common good of society. Even the island world of Tahiti could not dispense with sanctions against those members who did not play by its demographic rules. Diderot glosses over these cracks, though. Despite the moral strictures existing on Tahiti, he postulates in the heading of his story, it was a question of *actions physiques* which existed wholly outside the realm of *idées morales.*

In fact, woman is accorded no explicit special role in the utopian world of Tahiti, but the sanctions against permissive women, which are much more severe than the punishments intended for men, imply indirectly that the feminine had quite another function in a society whose existence and continuation depended on the means of securing descendants. Despite the author's intentions, *idées morales* clearly do emerge. The natural self-regulation of the utopian community is, in the final analysis, a moral one.[35] And this moral regulation consists largely in control over female sensuality.

All of the texts by Diderot discussed here suggest that this control was necessary for society. Even in the most natural of societies, woman's closeness to nature (i.e., her sexuality) requires an institution of control, in order to secure the biological reproduction of the species. In this context, Diderot accorded female modesty the decisive role. *One* important function of *morality* lay in just that channeling of female sexuality that we have already encountered as a decisive mark of woman's humanity in the *Encyclopédie*. In contrast to Diderot, who only treated this subject unconsciously, Rousseau regarded it as a central problem.

5

The Historical
and Moral-Philosophical
Dimensions of the Feminine

The texts dealt with up until now have viewed female nature as an
ahistorical entity. The relegation of woman to the realm of sensation, in
contrast to man's rational orientation, was justified by means of arguments from sensory physiology and epistemology. The centuries-old
"metaphysics of gender" in its specifically eighteenth-century version has
been thrown into relief against the background of the shift in epistemological paradigm.

One of the great achievements of the Enlightenment was, of course,
the conception of human nature as part of a universal natural history.[1]
The various attempts to explore the natural context of which human beings
formed a part extend from Helvétius, via d'Holbach, to Condorcet and
Rousseau, to name only the most important representatives of this anthropology. The abandonment of the Creation myth raised questions about
the *history* of human nature, and the answers were fed by the period's
numerous travel accounts. Eighteenth-century philosophers were confronted with a picture of the synchrony of the asynchronous. In their
efforts to reconstruct the history of humanity, they sought to place ex-
plorers' observations about peoples who were at a different stage of civilization from the Europeans into a comparative framework.[2]

Our subject raises the question of the role played by women in the
history of the path toward humanness or, in the terminology of the time,

of the "civilizing" of woman. Although the question seems both sensible and obvious, it has rarely been asked in a systematic fashion. This holds true both for eighteenth-century texts and for the secondary literature. Thus, in her fundamental work on eighteenth-century French anthropology Michèle Duchet adopts the ostensibly gender-neutral perspective of the texts she investigates.[3]

In the following I would like to show, by examining texts by Rousseau, that there is a specific historiography of female nature. The grounding of female sex-specific character in nature also historicizes nature itself. To be sure, this is not accomplished in the same manner as for the species "Man." Anthropological discourse only treats woman, and then often only implicitly, when her development and history diverge from that of man. As a result, the numerous conceptions of "female nature" appear, when separated from their anthropological contexts, as normative constructions. The treatment of Rousseau is typical here; the usual reaction to his image of woman is either indignation at such an act of patriarchal despotism or the view that it is founded solely on the socioeconomic necessities of bourgeois life.[4] I consider both explanations inadequate for understanding the great significance and model character that Rousseau's representations of women (Sophie, Julie) had for broad segments of the French public. *How* Rousseau's notion of femininity was connected to his general theories on the philosophy of history, and how precisely this notion lived on in the tradition, remains to be examined.

In fact, there are few explicit statements on the nature and natural history of woman in the two discourses[5] which lay the groundwork for Rousseau's anthropological theory. In contrast, chapter 5 of *Emile*, in which guidelines for the upbringing and education of Sophie are set down for the female sex as a whole, deals extensively with the subject of women. Rousseau proceeds from Sophie's training as a companion for Emile, whose upbringing as a man he described in detail in the preceding four chapters. At first, Sophie's upbringing seems aimed solely at making of her a submissive wife. Silvia Bovenschen has demonstrated that training for wifehood is symptomatic of the function of the feminine in the process of becoming human: "Woman represents, so to speak, the humus for the perfection of the human being—a phrase which must now be corrected to read: for the perfection of man."[6] Bovenschen sees the predefined destiny of Sophie/woman primarily as a "supplementary negation of male definitions." For her, "female nature," as it appears in Sophie, is not transmitted by means of the "central categories of [Rousseau's] philosophy of history" but rather is "only indirectly visible through male demands." The "feminine is absent from the genealogy of human history."[7] The female canon of virtues is, for her, merely derivative of the universal system of virtues.

In the following discussion I try to show that this seemingly obvious impression is misleading. The definitions of the feminine in Rousseau are not simply normative constructions. Rather, they derive their logic from the total context of his theory.

Control Over the Passions
as Educational Objective in *Emile*

One theme which we can follow through all of the tutor's advice for Sophie is the moderation of the girl's appetites, passions, and needs. All those qualities usually considered feminine, such as a fondness for finery, curiosity, coquetry, adroitness, and garrulousness, which Rousseau describes as "natural inclinations," must be channeled in order to prevent excess. Thus the fondness for finery must not end in extravagant spending; the girl's curiosity must not be indulged, lest she ask too many questions; her coquetry must remain within the bounds of propriety, and her adroitness and cunning must not lead to duplicity. One could cite many more of the examples used to underline the educational principle that only those girls develop into honorable and chaste women who are accustomed early, through "habitual restraint," to moderate their needs and to keep their moods constantly in check throughout their lives.[8]

Just as needs must not degenerate into passion, reason and knowledge must remain within strict boundaries. Rousseau not only regards women's intellectual potential as inferior to men's to begin with, he also considers the intentional development and encouragement of women's mental capacities unnatural. Girls and women cannot, and should not, progress beyond a certain stage of thinking. Their knowledge should be directed to concrete objects relating to their practical lives. It is not woman's role to think in abstract principles; her place, instead, is in the realm of the tangible:

> The search for abstract and speculative truths, for principles and axioms in science, for all that tends to wide generalisation, is beyond a woman's grasp; their studies should be thoroughly practical. It is their business to apply the

principles discovered by men, it is their place to make the observations which lead men to discover those principles. A woman's thoughts, beyond the range of her immediate duties, should be directed to the study of men, or the acquirement of that agreeable learning whose sole end is the formation of taste; for the works of genius are beyond her reach. . . .[9]

It is these aspects of girls' education that have led to an exclusively negative view of Rousseau's ideas and their dismissal as a "program of domestication" and *dressage*.

Women were not simply deficient, though. Rousseau also equipped them with an equal number of positive qualities. Men's strong suit, producing "works of the mind," was replaced in women by spontaneous observation and feeling. Female taste (*goût*) was the counterpart to male reason (*raison*). This contrast characteristically illuminates the dimensions of the female cognitive faculty. Taste applies to the realms of art and morality, serving to judge both the beautiful and the good. "Taste is formed partly by industry and partly by talent, and by its means the mind is unconsciously opened to the idea of beauty of every kind, till at length it attains to those moral ideas which are so closely related to beauty. Perhaps this is one reason why ideas of propriety and modesty are acquired earlier by girls than by boys. . . ."[10] For Rousseau *goût* is a particular means of understanding. Taste is not random or merely subjective, but contains a certain claim to truth. It remains, however, on the level of sensory knowledge and thus is only adequate to judge individual situations. Only male reason is equal to generalizations reaching beyond the immediate perceptions of the moment. In order to attain *goût*, girls require no intensive training or education. On the contrary, what characterizes taste is precisely its naturalness and immediacy. It presumes not acquired knowledge, but natural talent; rational thought is positively detrimental to taste. For this reason, Rousseau expressly opposes any intentional encouragement and instruction for girls. When it comes to artistic development, particularly singing and dancing, he argues against giving girls lessons. "Take the case of singing; does this art depend on reading music; cannot the voice be made true and flexible, can we not learn to sing with taste and even to play an accompaniment without knowing a note?"[11] The same applies to conversation, which he accords first place in the hierarchy of the "art of pleasing." He explicitly differentiates the male rhetorical tradition from women's innate linguistic talents. "A man says what he knows, a woman says what will please; the one needs knowledge, the other taste. . . ."[12] The transition from an aesthetic sense of taste to moral sentiment is fluid. In social life, as in the arts, woman behaves with the same simplicity, which is spontaneous and free of knowledge. She observes and "feels" her environment. Her behavior is not determined by principles, but by intuitive understanding. The passage in which Rousseau describes a host and hostess at a dinner party is typical. The man's social behavior is determined by information about the individual guests, the woman's by observation and sensitivity: "[T]he man knowing the assembled guests will place them according to his knowledge; the wife, without previous acquaintance, never makes a mistake; their looks and bearing have already shown her what is wanted and every one will find himself where he wishes to be."[13] This gift for observing people is not the fruit of training; it is innate to women. "Can this art be acquired? No; it is born with women; it is common to them all, and men never show it to the same degree. It is one of the distinctive characters of the sex."[14] It is this innate gift of observation which determines women's moral judgments and actions. Their social conduct is not mediated by (rationally based) principles and morality, but is a sort of perception of feelings. "The men will have a better philosophy of the human heart, but she will read more accurately in the heart of men. Woman should discover, so to speak, an experimental morality, man should reduce it to a system."[15] Equipped as she is by nature with a social instinct, woman is a more social being than man. For this reason she has a better command of the social graces and social intercourse than man. That which man has often acquired artificially, and which is therefore "insincere" springs from woman's natural character. "[A] woman's politeness is less insincere than ours, whatever we may think of her character; for she is only acting upon a fundamental instinct. . . ."[16] Rousseau traces this female nature back to specific biological functions—and the social functions that derive from them—in which man and woman differ fundamentally. Woman's duties of childbearing and childrearing, of maintaining a harmonious family life, demand particular social qualities: a restrained and moderate nature and, above all, gentleness, "what is most desired in a woman."[17]

This explanation, of course, does not go beyond a normative construction. There is no valid reason why these tasks could not be accomplished with the aid of knowledge acquired through a rationally based morality. In fact, a number of indicators in *Emile* might lead us to conclude that the necessity of a thorough separation between male and female sex-specific character rests on premises which precede its grounding in biological and social particularities, and that deriving Rousseau's representation of the feminine directly from his petty bourgeois social model does not go far enough. The point of departure for this consideration is my assertion that the dichotomy Rousseau sets up between untutored female taste on the one hand, and male knowledgeability on the other, correlates with another pair of opposites: utility and interest versus pleasure and complaisance. Thus in conjunction with his apology of female eloquence Rousseau suggests that, "utility should be the man's object; the woman speaks to give pleasure. There should be nothing in common but truth."[18] We find the disjunction between utility and complaisance elsewhere in *Emile*, in Book IV, where Rousseau explains the "Foundations of Taste" that the tutor is to convey to his pupil. Here, too, taste is clearly placed on the side of the nonutilitarian: "Taste deals only with things that are indifferent to us, or which affect at most our amusements, not those which relate to our needs; taste is not required to judge of these, appetite only is sufficient."[19] As a consequence, taste also only arises in the realm where diversion reigns. Only in "societies for amusement and idleness" (*sociétés d'amusements et d'oisiveté*)[20] can taste develop, for in business circles advantage (*l'intérest*), not pleasure, rules. Aesthetic enjoyment and judgment are thus evidently incompatible with the principle of utility, of purpose—or, more precisely—of advantage. Advantage, which in business circles inhibits enjoyment, also stands in the way of moral rectitude and friendliness:

> In social intercourse I observe that a man's politeness is usually more helpful and a woman's more caressing. This distinction is natural, not artificial. A man seeks to serve, a woman seeks to please. Hence a woman's politeness is less insincere than ours, whatever we may think of her character; for she is only acting upon a fundamental instinct; but when a man professes to put my interests before his own, I detect the falsehood, however disguised.[21]

The striving for advantage, egoism, which prevents man from fully developing taste as well as spontaneous charity, appears evidently not to affect woman's social behavior to such a great extent. Female politeness (*politesse*) remains natural and sincere because woman is less subject than man to the corrupting influences of the civilizing process. In contrast to man, egoistic passion in woman does not gain ascendancy over natural, instinctive politeness.

The instinctive character attributed to female sociability must be seen in connection with Enlightenment anthropology's orientation, as described earlier, toward natural history. The fact that human beings were regarded as natural beings had particular significance for female human beings, who, because of their function in biological reproduction, appeared more equipped with natural functions than male human beings.

Rousseau transferred this unequal attribution to the character of moral judgment. Here, as in the process of understanding, there was a shift of emphasis. If in the latter the part played by sensory perception was given greater weight, here a displacement occurred from rationally to emotionally based judgment. This shift resumes the tradition of sensualist aesthetics and moral philosophy dating back to the *querelle des anciens et des modernes* (Perrault and, in the eighteenth century, Cartaud de la Villate)[22] and runs parallel to the aestheticizing moral philosophy prevalent in England and Scotland (Shaftesbury, Hutcheson, Hume). As in this tradition, instinctive moral sensibility also fulfills a social function in Rousseau's moral philosophy and philosophy of history.[23] What was a mere tendency in moral philosophy is accentuated more in Rousseau's work, gaining a new gender-specific weight. The general tendency to situate human compassion in the private sphere—away from the goal-oriented world of business—is now expressed in the particular attribution of the moral qualities necessary for interpersonal relations to women, because their biological-social function brings them closer to the realm of the private.

Rousseau's position here seems decisive for all the further constructions that make up his image of woman. The category of egoism, which is used in *Emile* to explain the difference between male and female moral actions, is also central to Rousseau's social theory. An analysis of this category is the key to understanding his educational principles for Sophie and his representation of femininity more generally.

Egoism as the Competitive Society's Ruling Passion in the *Discours sur l'origine et les fondements de l'inégalité parmi les hommes*

The genesis of the feeling or, rather, the passion of egoism is the subject of Rousseau's 1755 *Discours sur l'origine et les fondements de l'inégalité parmi les hommes* (Discourse on the Origin and Foundations of the Inequality of Mankind) (Second Discourse). Self-interest (*amour-propre*) is the central category in Rousseau's considerations on the philosophy of history here. He views the origins of egoism in connection with a particular stage of civilization, the invention of metalworking and agriculture and, with them, of the division of labor and the emergence of private property. This epoch figures as the third stage in human history as constructed by Rousseau. In the original, premoral state of self-sufficient natural man (first stage), as well as in the golden age of communal living (second stage), the natural inequalities (strength, intelligence, age) still had no effect on social life. Once people began to claim land as their private property, however, which was a necessary consequence of agriculture, these inequalities led to social differences. In the course of the development of private property and economic competition new types of interests emerged. "In a word, there arose rivalry and competition on the one hand, and conflicting interests on the other, together with a secret desire on both of profiting at the expense of others. All these evils were the first effects of property, and the inseparable attendants of growing inequality."[24] Out of this change in property relations there followed a transformation in human motivations for action. The innate human instinct of self-preservation (*amour de soi*) was perverted into self-interest (*amour-propre*). Thus egoism was not an original human characteristic, as many earlier social philosophers had claimed (Hobbes, Locke, Mandeville). Instead, Rousseau regarded this passion as the result of particular social conditions, which gave human kindness no chance to develop. At the inception of socialization, in the golden age, the instinct of self-preservation was, accordingly, compatible with natural pity (*pitié naturelle*) because the interests of individuals were linked by common property ownership. Rousseau describes this stage as an idyll in which the moral and aesthetic feelings potentially present in all human beings could unfold:

> As ideas and feelings succeeded one another, and heart and head were brought into play, men continued to lay aside their original wildness; their private connections became every day more intimate as their limits extended. They accustomed themselves to assemble before their huts round a large tree; singing and dancing, the true offspring of love and leisure, became the amusement, or rather the occupation, of men and women thus assembled together with nothing else to do.[25]

This was, however, also the stage where the foundations of corruption were laid, and where the perfection of human capacities prepared for their later depravation.

The perfection of reason plays a decisive role in this process. Reason first perfects itself in the process of mastering nature through material labor:

> On the seashore and the banks of rivers, they invented the hook and line, and became fishermen and eaters of fish. In the forests they made bows and arrows, and became huntsmen and warriors. In cold countries they clothed themselves with the skins of the beasts they had slain. The lightning, a volcano, or some lucky chance acquainted them with fire, a new resource against the rigours of winter: they next learned how to preserve this element, then how to reproduce it, and finally how to prepare with it the flesh of animals which before they had eaten raw. This repeated relevance of various beings to himself, and one to another, would naturally give rise in the human mind to the perceptions of certain relations between them. Thus the relations which we denote by the terms great, small, strong, weak, swift, slow, fearful, bold, and the like, almost insensibly compared at need, must have at length produced in him a kind of reflection.[26]

This context is important because it makes clear the hidden underlying motives. Not merely the thirst for knowledge, but primarily physical necessity drove human beings to exercise their minds. Rousseau concurs with other philosophers of history in regarding physical needs as the first motor of reason.[27]

In the early stages these needs are communal ones. Reason serves the primitive commonweal. But reason, as just defined, only develops fully at a later stage, in which the partition of immediate needs into private interests begins. The human being only attains general concepts at the stage of agriculture and metalworking, which also means the period of private property. Thus as soon as it has reached a certain stage of development, reason begins to serve private purposes. The rationality of the individual begins to conflict with that of others. Reason is soon occupied not only with mastering nature, in order to make the earth habitable, but also, under conditions of competition, with securing advantage over one's fellow human beings. Human beings no longer think only with each other but also against each other. Reason becomes the handmaid of egoism, fusing with it into a single motive. It becomes "'calculating reason,' chained to the sensual passions."[28]

Rousseau criticizes this, but the union of reason and egoism makes such an impression on him that he equates one with the other. For him, the relationship between the two even appears to be reversed. At a developed stage of society the means becomes the cause: "It is reason that engenders *amour-propre*, and reflection that confirms it: it is reason which turns man's mind back upon itself, and divides him from everything that could disturb or afflict him. It is philosophy that isolates him, and bids him say, at sight of the misfortune of others: 'Perish if you will, I am secure.'"[29] In this reversal lies an insight that plays an important role in Rousseau's philosophy of history. According to this construction, not only do needs and interests further thought; rational understanding also affects needs: with increasing understanding new needs arise. Needs and reason interact, providing the point of departure for the dynamic of history.[30]

Through reason, finally, needs are transformed into those fatal "passions" that Rousseau criticizes:

> Whatever moralists may hold, the human understanding is greatly indebted to the passions, which, it is universally allowed, are also much indebted to the understanding. It is by the activity of the passions that our reason is improved; for we desire knowledge only because we wish to enjoy; and it is impossible to conceive any reason why a person who has neither fears nor desires should give himself the trouble of reasoning. The passions, again, originate in our wants, and their progress depends on that of our knowledge; for we cannot desire or fear anything, except from the idea we have of it, or from the simple impulses of nature. Now savage man, being destitute of every species of enlightenment, can have no passions save those of the latter kind: his desires never go beyond his physical wants.[31]

The History of Female Reason: The Golden Age in One's Own Home

It is only against the background of Rousseau's philosophy of history, as enunciated in the Second Discourse, that his criticism of female passion and reason becomes intelligible. When Rousseau seeks to prevent abstract thought and the development of needs into passions in women, it is not simply a matter of female socialization. The critique of female reason and passion is no mere "women's problem." What is at stake, rather, is the good of society as a whole, within which women are to fulfill a particular role. This role is defined according to the difficulties that, in Rousseau's view, the society faces.

Here we can see the inadequacy of an interpretation that views women's situation—whether in theory or in the social realities of the eighteenth century—in isolation. Gender relations do not suffice to explain the development of theoretical concepts about woman either. These opinions become interesting and illuminating, however, when viewed as components of a total theory of social development.

Woman evidently embodies a sphere of bourgeois society that must be spared the "war of all against all." It is the sphere that has not yet been penetrated by society's "perversions" and "alienations." Rousseau's theoretical strength is that he not only claims this for the present but explains it within his philosophy of history. It is precisely in those parts of his theory of human development where he expounds on the particular history of woman that it becomes clear the extent to which the portrayal of woman makes sense only within his general theory.

It thus remains to be shown that woman's depravation runs a different course from that of man. In the course of human development, female reason had evidently not been instrumentalized for competition in the way that male reason has. In the first phase of settlement, the pastoral age, the emergence of the family established a division of labor. The woman took over household work and tended the family. "The sexes, whose manner of life had been hitherto the same, began now to adopt different ways of living. The women became more sedentary, and accustomed themselves to mind the hut and their children, while the men went abroad in search of their common subsistence."[32] From then on human history became divided into a history of man and a history of woman—or so one might assume. In his account, however, Rousseau speaks only of *homme* in the gender-neutral sense. He does not explicitly follow woman from her emergence from the natural state to the first division of labor and the beginnings of a life different from man's, to her development into a civilized being, as he does for man. All that he gives us are a few hints and a history of man against which to contrast a possible history of woman. It seems clear to me though, that Rousseau, with his constant emphasis on the different natures of the sexes, proceeds from a divergent anthropology of the sexes as well, for the results of the development from "natural" to civilized woman are quite different from those of the development from "natural" to civilized man. Only the historical development of man is described in a systematic fashion, however. In contrast, he conceives of the historical dimension of the feminine only as a deviation from or negative side of male history. This aspect of human history must be reconstructed from the silences in Rousseau's account.

If we begin with the assumption that the ways of life of man and woman differed in the period of their first emergence from the state of nature, we may conclude that female cognition developed within another framework and under other conditions from that of men. Woman's capacity for thought develops not through hunting, war, or agriculture but, rather, within the microcosm of the family, where emotions unfold:

> The first expansions of the human heart were the effects of a novel situation, which united husbands and wives, fathers and children, under one roof. The habit of living together soon gave rise to the finest feelings known to humanity, conjugal love and paternal affection. Every family became a little society, the more united because liberty and reciprocal attachment were the only bonds of its union.[33]

The character of this "little society" did not change to the same extent as the world of men.

Entering the house of Sophie's parents, Emile encounters circumstances similar to those described for the golden age. Nevertheless, women evidently cannot escape the process of human depravation. The transformation of *amour de soi* into *amour-propre*, which characterizes the transition from the second state of nature to the state of civilization, also occurs in woman. The end point of this development, however, is not the egoistic businesswoman who cheats her competitors but the shameless lady of the Parisian aristocracy who no longer fulfills the duties of her sex. The trajectory must therefore be a different one from that followed by man. It is, apparently, not calculating, egoistic reason which makes women immoral.

Female reason does not develop to the same extent as man's. Sophie provides the best example: incapable of abstract thought, she remains on the level of the concrete and tangible, as we have seen. All women's attempts to use their intellectual capacities as men do are doomed to failure. Woman becomes a ridiculous caricature of the man she seeks to emulate.

> Outside her home she always makes herself ridiculous and she is very rightly a butt for criticism, as we always are when we try to escape from our own position into one for which we are unfitted. These highly talented women only get a hold over fools. We can always tell what artist or friend holds the pen or pencil when they are at work; we know what discreet man of letters dictates their oracles in private. This trickery is unworthy of a decent woman.[34]

To the extent, however, that woman remains excluded from male reasoning, her spontaneous feelings and compassion remain untouched by "alienation." Her "politeness" is more natural than man's, closer than

man's politeness to the original "goodness" of natural human beings.
While rational considerations often hinder man from acting compassion-
ately, woman acts spontaneously, unencumbered by "cold" reason.

Iring Fetscher has pointed out that Rousseau has a dual concept of
"reason": alongside the Hobbesian notion of egoistic calculation he includes a second meaning, *understanding* reason (i.e., moral reason),
which "leads to an understanding of the (beautiful and objectively reasonable) order"[35] and which allows civilized, depraved people to overcome their low sensual appetites and to put the common good before their
own interests. Both forms of moral action, that resting on the natural
"goodness" of natural human beings and that arising from understanding reason exist side by side in civilized society. "Alongside the higher
morality of virtue, Rousseau . . . also reserved a place in communal life
for unspectacular, instinctive 'bonté.' He did not trace moral life back to
a single principle, instead placing simple 'bonté' next to 'vertu.' . . ."[36]
These two forms of morality appear to me to be unevenly distributed
between the two sexes, however. While woman has retained premoral
goodness, man acts on the basis of rational understanding. This behavior requires him to struggle with his passions. It is precisely this process
of overcoming bad tendencies with rational understanding that characterizes Emile's "apprenticeship." Matters are different when it comes to
Sophie's upbringing. She is taught to be virtuous by constraint:

> They must be trained to bear the yoke from the first, so that they may not
> feel it, to master their own caprices and to submit themselves to the will of
> others. If they were always eager to be at work, they should sometimes be
> compelled to do nothing. Their childish faults, unchecked and unheeded, may
> easily lead to dissipation, frivolity and inconstancy. To guard against this,
> teach them above all things self-control.[37]

This rigorous training is apparently necessary in order to achieve in
girls through force and habit a conduct they could not attain through their
own understanding. If—as Rousseau asserts—man's ability is to set up
moral principles, then woman's is to follow them obediently. This absolute obedience compensates for woman's weakness, her tendency to fall
victim to the vices surrounding her, and her inability to control her passions by her own efforts. This does not mean that women's moral actions
proceed without any understanding reason whatsoever. It is precisely the
goal of virtuous behavior that Rousseau sees as the only justification for
training women's minds. When he speaks of the "art of thinking" in rela-

tion to women, it is always in the context of fulfilling their *moral* duties as wives and mothers: "[I]f a woman is quite unaccustomed to think, how can she bring up her children? How will she know what is good for them? How can she incline them to virtues of which she is ignorant, to merit of which she has no conception?"[38] He leaves no doubt in the reader's mind, however, that the necessity for even this most rudimentary training of women's minds is already the unwelcome consequence of humanity's depraved condition. Were it not for society's decadence, women would not require reason in order to be virtuous:

> I would not altogether blame those who would restrict a woman to the labours of her sex and would leave her in profound ignorance of everything else; but that would require a standard of morality at once very simple and very healthy, or a life withdrawn from the world. In great towns, among immoral men, such a woman would be too easily led astray; her virtue would too often be at the mercy of circumstances; in this age of philosophy, virtue must be able to resist temptation; she must know beforehand what she may hear and what she should think of it.[39]

Ultimately, however, women's understanding reason has its natural limits. Because of their underdeveloped moral understanding, women are helpless to resist the corruption of great cities, the very epitome of moral decay. "Women of Paris and London, forgive me! There may be miracles everywhere, but I am not aware of them; and if there is even one among you who is really pure in heart, I know nothing of our institutions."[40] Thus woman lacks both the egoistic reason to participate as man does in the process of social decay and its opposite, the higher moral understanding which could prevent this process of depravation. Like human beings in the state of nature, she is driven by her (premoral) desires and inclinations.

In woman's case, unlike man's, what regulates these instinctive inclinations is not reason but "modesty." Rousseau compares this female characteristic with the female animal's "negative instinct," thus underlining woman's primitive nature:

> The Most High has deigned to do honour to mankind; he has endowed man with boundless passions, together with a law to guide them, so that man may be alike free and self-controlled; though swayed by these passions man is endowed with reason by which to control them. Woman is also endowed with boundless passions; God has given her modesty to restrain them.[41]

Woman is more subject than man to drives that Rousseau likens to animal instincts. In this context he speaks of the "female of man" (*femelle de l'homme*).[42] The female sense of modesty—half natural drive, half "civilized" feeling—is the main determinant of female virtuousness. One may judge the depravation of the female sex according to the degree or absence of modesty, which corresponds to man's moral understanding reason. Man contains his passions through his capacity for reason, woman with the help of her *feeling* of modesty. The shameless woman represents the counterpart to the egoistic calculating man. Woman's depravation is the depravation of her modesty (*pudeur*).

Woman lives in a more primitive and natural manner than man. She continues to dwell, at least partially, in the premoral state of savages who could be neither good nor evil because they did not exist as social beings. To be sure, woman living in society is part of a community, but because of her biological role and the social role derived from it, she is closer than man to the immediately natural side of humanness. From this, Rousseau not only derives his well-known demands that her life be limited to the domestic-reproductive sphere. He also relegates the moral sex phylogenetically to a precivilized stage in which human beings still acted instinctively, a capacity that the state of civilization has destroyed. In his view, only elemental, animalistic expression could ensure the human qualities necessary to the family sphere. Rousseau intentionally writes of woman's "inclination" (*goût*), not of her "virtue" (*vertu*), when discussing her duties within the family, whereby the term *goût* is intended to signal greater primitivity, in conscious contrast to the rationally formed *vertu*: "What loving care is required to preserve a united family! And there should be no question of virtue in all this, it must be a labour of love, without which the human race would be doomed to extinction."[43] Rousseau creates the paradoxical situation in which woman living in seclusion, and devoting herself solely to the family, becomes the incarnation of nonegoistic action and thought. To the extent that human compassion is banished from the public sphere to the familial, private sphere, it takes up residence in a genuinely nonsocietal realm, woman's biological nature.   ·

His phylogenetic classification of woman not only makes Rousseau's aim of keeping her in relative ignorance seem logical; it also offers an explanation for the systematic curbing of woman's passionate nature to which I referred at the beginning of this chapter. In Sophie Rousseau recovers the lost golden age, that stage of human history when property was held in common and human beings lived in harmony with one another and nature. We find in her the anthropological qualities of humanity at the first stage of socialization.

When Emile and his tutor leave Paris like "knights-errant"[44] and move on to the provinces to look for a suitable spouse, they are also embarking on a journey into mankind's past, in search of human nature that has not yet been corrupted.

To describe this process of relegating woman to an earlier stage of civilization as a "domestication program"[45] is tautological. Against the background of Rousseau's anthropological assumptions, however, astonishing parallels appear between the development of the sexes in the course of individual and collective histories. Phylogenetically, the emergence of the passions runs parallel to the alienation of human beings from their original nature. The passions arise from and accompany human egoism. Rousseau speaks of

> man in the state of society, for whom first necessities have to be provided, and then superfluities; delicacies follow next, then immense wealth, then subjects, and then slaves. He enjoys not a moment's relaxation; and what is yet stranger, the less natural and pressing his wants, the more headstrong are his passions, and still worse, the more he has it in his power to gratify them; so that after a long course of prosperity, after having swallowed up treasures and ruined multitudes, the hero ends up by cutting every throat till he finds himself, at last, sole master of the world. Such is in miniature the moral picture, if not of human life, at least of the secret pretensions of the heart of civilized man.[46]

It is against this background that we must reevaluate the rules set down for Sophie's upbringing. Rousseau's attempt to organize the girl's education in such a way that her passions have no opportunity to develop in the first place expresses his objective of leaving woman in a stage of relative savagery that humanity, or rather its male component, has long since left behind. Silvia Bovenschen's argument that Rousseau denies woman the capacity for perfection[47] should be modified to read that this capacity, which he recognized as a permanent danger, should be inhibited. He fixes woman at a particular stage of human historical development, the second stage of the state of nature, the precivilized phase of the golden age. This stage was the precondition for the later depravation of the human race, and this depravation occurred, as Rousseau shows in the *Second Discourse*, with a dynamic of its own inherent to human perfectibility. To halt this dynamic was, it appears, a difficult undertaking,

as the "attacks" on Ninon de Lenclos and other learned women demonstrate.[48] Force is necessary for the creation of conditions under which
capacities—women's included—are inhibited from further development,
that is, from becoming perverted. The motto of Sophie's upbringing as a
woman, "desire mediocrity in all things,"[49] points to the structures set up
to contain development. Scarcely a theoretician of the eighteenth century
formulated as vehemently as Rousseau the demand that the development
of female personality be thwarted, because no other thinker saw so clearly,
or felt so keenly, the negative consequences of the competitive society.

The exercise of force, which marks girls' education in contrast to boys',
is a sign of woman's immaturity, an immaturity born of the anachronis-
tic character of the nature Rousseau's system attributes to her. As a "being
from another time" she is in no position to brave the adversities of the
depraved society. Thence her dependence on man, who possesses the
capacity for moral action based on rational understanding. Only in a protected space like the golden age can her instinctively good nature unfold.
When, however, woman is allowed to develop her natural inclinations,
it is—and this is significant—with a moral power far surpassing man's
reason-based morality. Only woman's less civilized moral sensibility can
create human ties in a strife-ridden society. Without her spontaneous
humanity all male rational considerations would come to nought. This
requires an environment, however, in which woman's natural feelings
have not already been perverted.

Rousseau creates this situation fictionally in *Julie, ou La Nouvelle
Héloïse*. Clarens, the community established by Wolmar, is a golden age
island in the midst of a depraved civilization. It is the subject of the rest
of the chapter.

The Return of the Golden Age in *La Nouvelle Héloïse*

In 1761, six years after the *Second Discourse*, Rousseau's only novel
La Nouvelle Héloïse, appeared. In Part IV of this epistolary novel he
designs an ideal social community, the country estate of Clarens, which
can be seen as the positive answer to the critique of society offered in his
two discourses. By looking at the way Clarens functions, I would like in
the following section to trace Julie's role within this utopian society, a
role intended by the author as a model, and thus of exemplary significance for the place of the feminine in his thought.[50]

Clarens functions as a self-sufficient community. Wolmar's intelligent and intensive farming methods guarantee a life of comfort—but not luxury!—based solely on the community's closed economic circulation. This economic self-sufficiency is emphasized by the geographical location of Clarens, which, enclosed by Lake Geneva and the mountains, appears as an inhabited island amidst virgin nature.[51] In the particular location and self-sufficient existence of Clarens, Rousseau constructs—as he did in the state of nature in the Second Discourse—a field of (literary) experimentation in which to develop his notions of an ideal-typical community.

Economic self-sufficiency is paradigmatic of Rousseau's economic ideas more generally.[52] Rejecting mercantilist notions, he believes that wealth rests on self-made products alone. All the necessities of life are produced on the estate. There is no systematic exchange with the outside world. Trade is reduced to an absolute minimum and consists almost entirely of barter:

> The great secret of our riches . . . is to have little money, and to avoid as far as possible, in using our goods, intermediate exchanges between the product and its use. No such exchange can be made without loss, and these losses, multiplied, reduce to almost nothing a moderate fortune, just as a junk dealer turns a fine golden box into a paltry trinket. We avoid the transport of our goods by using them on site, and avoid exchange by consuming them in kind, and in the indispensible conversion of that of which we have too much into that which we lack, we seek real exchanges where the convenience of each party serves to profit both, instead of sales and purchases for money which double the losses.[53]

The inhabitants of Clarens live in harmony with nature; by living self-sufficiently and shielding themselves from the deleterious effects of refined civilized existence, they have recovered the golden age on a higher plane. For Rousseau the progress of civilization (i.e., of scholarship and of the crafts) signifies a progress in human depravation. At Clarens there is thus no progress of this kind. Wolmar's achievement is the maintenance of the status quo, that is, not increasing production beyond the requirements of "natural needs." These needs are a bulwark against human beings' alienation from their true nature. In preventing money exchange, Wolmar also eliminates commodity production. The economy of Clarens is devoted exclusively to producing articles necessary for the daily use of community members:

Consider, finally, that an abundance of necessities cannot degenerate into abuse, because necessity has its natural measure, and true needs know no excess. One may spend as much on one suit of clothes as on twenty, and eat at one meal the produce of a year, but one cannot wear two suits of clothes at the same time or have dinner twice in one day. Thus opinion is unlimited, while nature everywhere encounters limits, and he of modest means who contents himself with well-being runs no risk of ruin.[54]

Wolmar protects his property against decay, which means both the slide into unproductivity and integration into a larger socially mediated system of exchange. Saint-Preux summarizes his reflections on Clarens thus: "[C]ontent with their fortune they do not seek to increase it for their children, but rather to leave them with the legacy they received, lands in good condition, devoted servants, a taste for work, order, moderation and everything that may render sweet and charming to sensible people the enjoyment of modest means, as well-conserved as they were honestly acquired."[55] Control over physical wants and their restriction to a natural measure are the principles according to which Wolmar runs Clarens. They ensure that the inherent human instinct of self-preservation does not degenerate into selfishness. The law of the accumulation of wealth has been repealed. The social immobility of the community corresponds to this stable and constant equilibrium between human beings and nature. The fact that nobody becomes rich ensures that nobody will aspire to leave his appointed place. "Each, finding in his own station in life everything he needs to be content, and not desiring to leave it, attaches himself to his station as though he were to stay there all his life, and the only ambition one retains is that of performing the duties of one's station well."[56] Since competition among members of the Clarens community has been banished, the master–servant relationship is transformed into one of patriarchal devotion. Saint-Preux, who explains Clarens to his confidant Milord Edouard in the tenth letter of Part IV, likens the relationship between masters and servants to that between parents and children. "Am I wrong, Milord, to compare such beloved masters to fathers and their servants to their children? You see that this is how they regard themselves."[57] The economic interests of day laborers, so Rousseau would have us believe, play only a minor role in their productivity. A more important and decisive motivation for their work at Clarens is devotion to their masters. Thus investment in the estate is also—and decisively— emotional, and it is woman who bears the main responsibility for this aspect of life:

Nonetheless an even more effective means, the only one economic considerations do not allow as a possibility, and which belongs more to Mad^e de
Wolmar, is to win the affection of these good people by granting them hers.
She does not believe that she can repay with money the efforts made on her
behalf, and feels that she owes a service to anybody who has done her one.
Laborers, servants, all those who have served her, if only for a day, become
her children. She participates in their pleasures, their pains, their fate; she
informs herself about their affairs; their interests are her own. She takes on a
thousand cares for them, giving them advice, settling their differences, and
shows them the amiability of her character not with honeyed, ineffective
words, but with true services and continual acts of kindness.[58]

At Clarens, the spheres of economic interest and emotional ties, separate
in civil society, are united. Family feeling goes beyond the family to
encompass the entire economic unit. Relations between masters and farm
servants approximate those between parents and children; relations between servants are described as those of siblings. Despite its scale, which
extends well beyond family members, work on the estate maintains its
quality of a household economy. Clarens still represents the "whole
house" (*oikos*) in which household and business are not yet separated from
each other.[59]

This unity corresponds to a single standard of morality, which is not
divided into a morality of work and a morality of private life. The hon-
esty (*franchise*) prevailing at Clarens is contrasted to the hypocrisy
Rousseau laments in his two discourses. Here there is no double standard, either in the literal or the figurative sense. Nobody has secrets from
anybody else, all present themselves as they really are. Absolute open-
ness is held up as the most important quality of human relationships. All
reveal their feelings to each other.[60] The compulsion to dissemble, which
exists both in courtly life and in the bourgeois world of business, has no
objective basis at Clarens, because all members are unified by a harmony
of interests.

I would like to take a closer look at the moral aspect of life at Clarens,
which appears to me closely interwoven with economic practice. Parallel to the economic microcosm of Clarens there is also a moral microcosm, which must be regarded as both consequence and cause of the
unusual circumstances prevailing there. Economic self-sufficiency has
its counterpart in the moral realm, which I would like to call *moral self-
sufficiency*. Rousseau emphasizes at several points that particular virtues
can only develop within the protected world of Wolmar's estate, secluded

from the outside world. The community watches over morality by constantly constructing a barrier against hostile outside influences. Just as
they avoid trade with their (urban) surroundings, in order not to destroy
their subsistence economy, they also view social contacts with city dwellers
as detrimental. This becomes particularly clear in the novel's treatment
of personal servants. In literature, servant figures are frequently used to
portray urban customs and morals. The master's frivolity, it seems, is
always reflected as a matter of course in his servant. Rousseau adopts
this cliché. As a result, no servants from outside Wolmar's sphere of
influence are hired to work at Clarens:

> Here they do not follow the maxim I have seen reigning in Paris and Lon-
> don, of choosing domestic servants who are already fully trained, that is, fully
> fledged scoundrels, those runners from one position to the next who adopt in
> each house through which they pass the faults of valets and masters, and make
> a practice of serving everyone, but attaching themselves to no one. Neither
> honesty, nor loyalty, nor zeal can be found among such persons, and this
> bunch of rascals ruins the master and corrupts the children in all wealthy
> houses.[61]

Furthermore, the masters of the house take a number of precautionary
measures to keep servants from spending their leisure time outside the
estate. Dances, entertainments, and games are organized to prevent the
moral decay emanating from the *cabarets*. Even the children's govern-
ess is a "simple and credulous, but attentive, patient and clever peasant
woman." Saint-Preux concludes that "they have spared nothing to prevent the vices of the city from penetrating a house whose masters neither have them, nor suffer them in others."[62]

This conscious seclusion from the outside world is based on the life
experiences of the inhabitants of Clarens. All members of the community—except Julie!—have chosen to stay in Clarens in order to distance
themselves from their previous lives. They have lived in the most di-
verse social circles in various places—Saint-Preux has even traveled
around the world—but without finding the inner peace they hope that
life in Clarens will bring them. A recognition that the world is evil is,
however, the precondition for an individual's acceptance at Clarens.
In order to live in the community, they must first reject society. Mov-
ing to Clarens entails not merely a change of place; it signifies a change
from the corrupt world of the aristocratic and bourgeois struggle for

survival to the intact world of peaceful communal life among like-minded people. Those who live at Clarens have been purified by their own experiences.[63]

Settlement at Clarens as the high point of a life, the end of a long development, in the course of which the soul has undergone purification—all this smacks of a secular return to Paradise. This construction is based on Rousseau's notion that progressive human corruption can only be halted by reflection on, and a return to, true (i.e., original) human nature. This process takes place at Clarens. When defending his economic methods, Wolmar invokes human beings' "natural needs." These must be continually differentiated from artificial, socially produced needs in order to prevent the slide into luxury production and consumption.

We find this principle of need reduction duplicated in the moral sphere. The physical needs regulating economic life have their counterpart in the "natural feelings" (*sentiments naturels*) or "natural passions" (*passions naturelles*), which are contrasted with the artificially created feelings and passions.[64] Control over material production corresponds to control over feelings, passions, and perceptions. Julie's use of the "Apollo Hall" is characteristic. This room, which is particularly pleasant, and whose particular location and cosy character produce an unusually intimate atmosphere, is seldom used. Julie's justification for this regulation is that "it would be much too pleasant" and that "the surfeit of comfort is, in the end, the most disagreeable of all." The commodification of articles of everyday use is congruent with the commodification of comforts. Only through abstinence can one achieve full enjoyment. When Claire praises the wise way of life of the inhabitants of Geneva in a letter to Julie, mentioning the distant relationships between husbands and wives in particular, it is also a reference to the spirit prevailing at Clarens. Here, too, living and working spheres are strictly separated along gender lines. While this separation is justified in the case of the servants as a means of ensuring virtuous conduct, in the case of the masters Rousseau makes an argument based on natural law:

> [S]he [Julie] maintains that the continual commerce of the sexes is based neither on love nor on the marriage bond. According to her, wife and husband are destined to live together, to be sure, but not in the same way; they must act in concert without doing the same things. A life that delights the one, she says, is unbearable to the other; the inclinations bestowed upon them by nature are as different as the functions she imposes upon them; their amuse-

ments are as different as their duties; in a word, the two work towards their common happiness along different paths, and this sharing of labor and cares is the strongest tie of their union.[65]

Claire, who makes similar observations in Geneva, concludes:

Your system is well confirmed here. The two sexes benefit in many ways from occupying themselves with different work and pastimes, which prevents their becoming bored with each other and ensures that they reunite with more pleasure. Thus is the sage's pleasure sharpened: abstain to heighten enjoyment is your philosophy; it is the Epicureanism of reason.[66]

This "philosophy" rests on the principle of controlling the passions. In order to reach the state of lasting happiness as it exists at Clarens, the grand passions, which soon cool, must be transformed into gentle but more lasting emotions. This is the key to Julie's happiness. Although she does not love Wolmar with the same passion as she once loved Saint-Preux, she is happy in her marriage to him. As she informs Saint-Preux, "Love is accompanied by a continual restlessness of jealousy or privation, ill-suited to marriage, which is a state of enjoyment and peace."[67] Love, like all grand passions, does not last long:

No passion produces such illusions as love. One takes its violence for a sign of its durability. The heart, overfull of such sweet emotion, projects it, so to speak, into the future, and as long as this love lasts one believes it will never end. Quite the contrary is the case, however; it is consumed by its very ardor; it declines along with youth, it fades along with beauty, it is extinguished by the frosts of age, and since the world began two white-haired lovers have never been seen sighing for each other.[68]

From the perspective of Clarens, love as passionate projection, an image we also find in *Emile,* appears as an illness. Julie speaks of wanting to cure Saint-Preux, referring implicitly to her own "cure," initiated by Wolmar, which freed her from the error of believing that only passionate love (*amour-passion*) could bring true happiness.[69]

Wolmar also sets in motion this process of moral purification in Saint-Preux: "My successes encouraged me, and I wanted to attempt to heal you as well, just as I had healed her."[70] Saint-Preux's continuation as a teacher at Clarens depends on the success of this attempt. Wolmar already knows the stages Saint-Preux will need to pass through in his development. He plans, in step-by-step "therapy," to disabuse him of the illusion that Madame de Wolmar is still his beloved Julie:

> Instead of his mistress I force him to see always the wife of an honest man and the mother of my children: I replace one picture with another, covering the past with the present. One takes a skittish horse up to the object which frightens it, until it is no longer afraid. One must do the same with young people whose imaginations still burn when their hearts have already cooled, showing them monsters in the distance which disappear when approached.[71]

Wolmar's task is to transform the love between Julie and Saint-Preux, the element with the greatest potential to disturb the collective happiness of Clarens, into a friendship. With the gift for cool reflection inherent in his own dispassionate nature he regulates the passions as he does his estate. He may be considered the creator of the spirit of Clarens. It is he who sets up in programmatic form not only the principles ruling economic life there but also communal social life, and who creates the preconditions for their realization. The purification of Julie's and Saint-Preux' passions is his work.[72] "Could we ever have come this far by our own efforts?" asks Julie at the end of this evolution—at a point when she realizes that "this is the first time in my life when I can write to you without fear or shame," only to answer her own question: "Never, never my good friend; the mere attempt would have been audacity. . . . I saw your sensitive heart, filled with the acts of generosity of the best of men, imbued with love for him."[73] In the end it is Wolmar who engineers Saint-Preux's reunion with Julie and decides to hire him as a tutor.

The Function of the Feminine in the Utopia of Clarens

What was Julie's function in the constellation of Clarens, or, more generally, the function of the feminine in this ideal utopian situation? In *Emile*, as I have tried to show, the feminine represents the ethical values of the golden age in the midst of a depraved civilization. By her very nature, woman brings *homme naturel*'s spontaneous natural sympathy into a society whose members no longer live for, but rather against, each other. In Clarens, in contrast, the separation of male and female life principles appears to have broken down. The harmonious coexistence of all members functions without the selfish behavior of individuals at the expense of the community. Wolmar, too, possesses the feminine virtues paradigmatically displayed in *Emile*. It is he who brought about the return of his self-sufficient estate to the precivilized golden age. He appears as

Julie's true preceptor; Rousseau accords her no active role. Julie's moral uniqueness, as expressed in the letters of the other members, appears at first as a paradox.

In order to explain this peculiarity, one must take into account that Rousseau is thinking of Clarens' *inception*, even if the state he describes is presented as a final one. Clarens appears as an ideal final stage, whose specificity lies in its very stasis, in the impossibility of further development. He does, however, describe the road which led there in the novel's first three parts. The two central protagonists and representatives of the "Clarens principle," Julie and Wolmar, arrive there by different routes. Wolmar has been forced by outer circumstances to build a new life for himself. His extensive experience of life and thoroughly virtuous character lead him to choose the economic methods just described. His renunciation of profitable market-oriented surplus production rests on his insight into the unfortunate autodynamics of capitalist business methods. Wolmar creates conditions which do not permit the perversions of *amour de soi* described in the Second Discourse. Julie's case is a different one. For her, it is only the conditions created by Wolmar that allow her to be virtuous. While Wolmar places his reason in the service of his moral sentiments and rejects the selfish way of life of those around him of his own volition, Julie is unable to create the preconditions for her own virtuousness. She marries Wolmar against her will, and Clarens is the realization of Wolmar's ideal of social life, whose wisdom she comes to understand only gradually. It is against this background that her development begins.

This break becomes visible in the separation of her person into Julie d'Etanges and Mme de Wolmar. Marriage marks the beginning of the development of her moral capacities and not, as in Wolmar's case, its culmination. The recognition that Mme de Wolmar is no longer identical to Julie d'Etanges is the crucial experience that allows Saint-Preux to overcome his passion and live in friendship with his former lover. The reality of the married woman replaces the image of the lover in his mind. While the memory of Julie arouses fantasies of passion, the lived reality of Mme de Wolmar evokes calm and peace. Saint-Preux experiences this metamorphosis for the first time in the *Elisée*, the artificial garden created by Julie: "I thought I saw the picture of virtue where I sought that of pleasure. That image became confused in my mind with the features of Mad^e de Wolmar, and for the first time since my return I saw Julie in her absence not as she once was for me, and as I still love to imagine her, but as she appears before my eyes every day."[74]

I have shown that this process was set in motion by Wolmar. He is omnipresent in Saint-Preux's meditations: "I thought I saw his intelligent, piercing eye looking into my innermost heart, making me blush with shame once again."[75] But it is the presence of Mme de Wolmar that finally brings this purification process to a successful conclusion. She is the incarnation of Wolmar's principles. Herein lies her uniqueness, which at the same time underlines the specificity and function of the feminine within the novel. Only the experience of her lived virtue allows Saint-Preux himself to follow Wolmar's moral commandments. The figure of Mme de Wolmar enables him to experience the moral code prevailing at Clarens as true happiness, in contrast to which sexual love reveals itself as "aberrant fantasy" (*écarts d'imagination*) and the "base transports of an illicit passion" (*vils transports d'une passion criminelle*). It is Mme de Wolmar's presence that first allows Saint-Preux to experience the *pleasure* of virtue (*la jouissance de la vertu*), which Wolmar had only conveyed through precepts.[76] Wolmar holds influence over Saint-Preux's rational understanding, but it is only through Mme de Wolmar that this process of understanding becomes a moral sentiment, and thus relevant for concrete practice. The virtuous woman's presence is indispensable for the durability of this sentiment, and it alone can suppress the passions of years gone by. "When the formidable Julie pursues me, I take refuge in the company of Madame de Wolmar, and I find peace. Where would I flee to if this asylum were taken away? All times, all places are dangerous when I am far from her."[77] Saint-Preux feels himself a man divided. The struggle between virtue and passion runs straight through his person. He does not have the power within himself to overcome the "unrest of the passions." "In truth, Julie, I believe that I have two souls; you keep the good one as a pawn in your hands."[78] Woman is the center of virtue. Her own person breathes life into the Clarens philosophy. She can do this because the process of moral insight occurs in her neither as a rational act (as in the case of Wolmar) nor as the struggle between two opposing souls (as in the case of Saint-Preux) but, rather, as a spontaneous sympathetic understanding of the moral climate of Clarens. Her virtuousness does not result from effort but, rather, from the realization and development of her nature. She is the only person at Clarens who does not choose seclusion out of a painful experience of life in society. The ad-

vantages of Clarens are not revealed to her in contrast to "outside," as is
the case for Wolmar and Saint-Preux but, rather, arouse a natural reso-
nance in her heart. Clarens is, as it were, the materialization of her inner
nature. The tension between the production of luxury items and articles
of everyday use, moderation and excess, passion and virtue, sympathy
and egoism marks both Wolmar and Saint-Preux, if in different ways.
Both must master this tension through continual exertion: Wolmar in his
economic considerations, Saint-Preux in the repression of the fantasies
which continually overtake him. Julie knows no such dichotomy. She is
the harmony of Clarens, and is for this reason better able to realize it even
than Wolmar. This becomes apparent when we look at the place which
has been shaped by her alone: the Elisée, that spot where Saint-Preux's
"conversion" from lover to virtuous friend takes place.

In contrast to the estate of Clarens, whose well-ordered economy is
always presented as the result of Wolmar's continual exertions, the
Elisée appears as a work of nature. Wolmar's (agri)cultural achievements do not extend to this precisely circumscribed part of the former
orchard. The Elisée exists in a natural, precivilized state, comparable
to that of the South Sea islands.[79] Visitors to the Elisée feel themselves
transported back to the beginnings of humanity: "I believed I was seeing the most savage, the most solitary place in nature, and I felt that I
was the first mortal ever to penetrate this wilderness."[80] But that which
appeared primitive and untouched by human hands was created by Julie.
The Elisée is her work; it is the only place in Clarens not subject to
Wolmar's management. On the contrary, in the Elisée it is Wolmar who
works under Julie's direction. In contrast to the rest of the estate, however, which testifies to Wolmar's circumspect management, in the Elisée
all traces of human labor have been effaced. Here Julie reconstructs
the long-conquered savage state of nature. Only here is a perfect harmony of humankind and nature achieved. The peaceful atmosphere of
the estate finds its fullest expression in the part "cultivated" by Julie.
She manages effortlessly, naturally, and unconsciously what Wolmar
has only achieved after years of discipline and planning. Her work does
not bear the imprint of labor; the role of "administratrix" is an emana-
tion of her own nature and not, like Wolmar's estate management, the
conscious exercise of a function. Julie's activity, like the vegetation of
the Elisée, is akin to a natural force unfolding within the external circumstances created by Wolmar. Julie creates the primitive state of nature; Wolmar only approaches it in limiting the excesses of civiliza-

tion. This also becomes apparent in the differing functions of the Elisée and the rest of the estate. In contrast to the rest of Clarens, the Elisée is not cultivated according to the principle of maximum efficiency but rather only that of agreeableness and pleasure. The yield of fruits is merely a by-product:

> [O]nly in this one place has the useful been sacrificed to the agreeable, and in the rest of the lands one has taken such care with the plants and trees that even with one less orchard the harvest of fruits does not cease to be greater than before. If you imagine how happy one is sometimes to see wild fruits in the depths of the forest, and even to partake of them, you will understand the pleasure of finding in this artificial wilderness excellent and ripe, if sparse and unattractive, fruits, which in turn affords the pleasure of collecting and choosing them.[81]

Here we find the same juxtaposition of utility (*utilité*) and agreeableness (*agrément/plaisir*) we encountered in the Second Discourse. Primitive nature in its savage state resists systematic exploitation, which is, in turn, the precondition for the complete harmony prevailing there. The danger of egoistic production is still inherent in Wolmar's economy, and he can only banish it by constant efforts to regulate needs. In Julie's world, in contrast, it appears fundamentally excluded. In the Elisée, the ideal utopian state, which Clarens can only approach, becomes reality.

James F. Jones regards the portrayal of the Elisée as only a "textual intensification"[82] of the world of Clarens, a microcosm reflecting Clarens in condensed form. The Elisée seems to have a wider significance, however. It embodies the world of woman in which—in contrast to the male world of work—Rousseau's utopian program of social harmony is more perfectly realized. This difference, however, is not merely gradual, as Jones would have it. Instead, it points to the fundamental differences Rousseau sets up between the female and male life principles. Female nature is more natural than male nature. Assuming that external circumstances do not inhibit her development, woman does intuitively what man does consciously, following his enlightened reason. Woman is incapable of creating these conditions by her own efforts; she depends on male preparations. Julie is confronted with conditions at Clarens, but she is not the mere executrix of Wolmar's philosophy of life. Rather, she is the stabilizing factor in the world of Clarens. Jones correctly points out the cracks in the edifice of Clarens, such as the discussion of disciplining domestic servants. It is no accident that Julie is responsible for mediating such conflicts when they arise. She embodies perfectly the social harmony which Wolmar's sense of justice can never approach. The utopian moment of Clarens, which Jones analyzes as the novel's principal element, is most fully realized in the person of Julie.

6

The Female Reduced
to Natural Instinct

While Rousseau scarcely presented the history of female nature explicitly, his successors attempted to distinguish the male and female components of the non-gender-specific construction *homme naturel*. In the 1780s
Choderlos de Laclos wrote three essays that were collected under the title
of the second, *Des femmes et de leur éducation* (On Women and Their
Education).[1] This second essay is the fragmentary answer to a prize question set by the Academy of Châlons-sur-Marne. Laclos is interesting in
the context of my analysis of Rousseau because, nearly thirty years after
the discourses, he proposes to draw conclusions for the history of woman
from Rousseau's social critique. The prize question had asked the best
means of improving women's education, a question characteristic of the
age's general and gender-specific interest in pedagogical issues. Laclos
answered, with a radicality that the Academy doubtless neither envisioned
nor intended: "There is no means of improving women's education."[2]
His reasoning rests on a particular definition of education: the development of human capabilities for the common good. "Either the word education has no meaning whatsoever, or one must understand it as the development of the faculties of the individual being educated, and their
direction towards social usefulness."[3] Because woman is the slave of man
in all societies, she cannot be educated in the sense just cited, for "wher-
ever slavery exists, there can be no education."[4]

Laclos elaborates on his notion of the enslavement of the female sex
in *Des Femmes et de leur éducation*. Here he attempts to apply Rousseau's

Second Discourse to the history of woman's humanness. Human beings, according to Laclos, are free by nature. The state of society, however, necessarily makes of them masters and slaves. Here, natural inequalities become social inequalities. These social differences, however—and here Laclos departs from Rousseau—are closely connected to sexual difference. Woman can be oppressed by man because she is physically weaker than him. He rejects Rousseau's notion that women also participated in the transition from a state of nature to a state of society. For Laclos, women were forced during the first stage of socialization to live with men. They never agreed to the social contract voluntarily. "The first woman who yielded to force or persuasion forged the chains of her entire sex."[5]

As land became men's property, so did women. Women lost their freedom with the abolition of communal property. Over the centuries they performed arduous tasks like beasts of burden. It was this experience of suffering which led the female sex to develop other faculties to compensate for their physical weakness: dexterity and the art of seduction. Women found that erotic enjoyment lived primarily from fantasy. They thus had to feed men's imaginations.

> Having acknowledged these initial truths, they learned first to veil their charms in order to arouse curiosity; they practiced the tedious art of refusing, even when they longed to consent; from this moment on they knew how to inflame the imagination of men, they knew how to awaken and guide desire as they pleased, thus were beauty and love born. Women's lot became gentler; although they did not succeed in freeing themselves entirely from the oppressed state to which their weakness condemns them; but in the state of perpetual warfare existing between them and men, one sees them, armed with the caresses they created, in ceaseless combat, sometimes conquering and often, more cleverly still, taking advantage of the forces directed against them.[6]

Laclos refers to female rule, a well-worn topos in contemporary characterizations of elegant Parisian society, as a particular form of the centuries-old enslavement of woman. In so doing he criticizes the theorists of progress, particularly Buffon, whom he addresses explicitly.

Inspired by his readings of contemporary travel accounts, Buffon proceeds from the assumption that human beings were intended by nature to live in communities. It was a characteristic of primitive societies that gender relations were marked by force. The undeveloped moral sentiments of people in primitive cultures, and the necessity of using violence to satisfy basic needs, led to the forceful subjection of woman to man, which was expressed in the fact that she performed the hardest physical labor. Sexual desire was underdeveloped in savages, only unfolding at a stage when basic needs were easier to satisfy. Only with desire did sociability and moral sensibility arise. Women exercised a greater influence over men's behavior and civilized male manners, which were based on brute strength. In a more advanced state of society, this made them men's equal partners.

> It is only among nations civilized to the point of politeness that women have obtained this equality of condition that is nevertheless so natural and so necessary for making a society pleasant: this politeness of manners is also their work; they have opposed the force of victorious arms, teaching us by their modesty to acknowledge the influence of beauty, which represents a greater natural advantage than strength. . . .[7]

Laclos and Buffon proceed from similar claims. Their conclusions are quite different, however. While Buffon views men's desire for women as the yardstick of a culture's development toward civilization and emancipation, for Laclos women's erotic attractiveness was only the most highly developed form of female oppression and slavery. For him woman's depravation is a double one: As the victim of man's lust for power, she is prevented from freely developing her own powers. This oppression leads to the stunting of her intellect and, in a second stage, to moral decay. In order to make her situation bearable, she is compelled to use deception in order to nourish in man the expectation of happiness, which she promises to fulfill.

It is no accident that Laclos did not create a female character in *Les Liaisons dangereuses* who, like Julie in *La Nouvelle Héloïse*, preserves the virtues of uncorrupted humanity, finding her happiness in them. On the contrary, we find the moral misery of an entire social stratum virtually compressed into the person of the Marquise de Merteuil. The seducer's cynical disregard for human feelings is redoubled and intensified by the Marquise's betrayal of the betrayer. Civilized manners, celebrated by Buffon as women's creation, are for Laclos the terrible height of woman's estrangement from true female nature. Social woman (*femme sociale*) is a paradigm for the moral decline of the human race.

Laclos sets up an opposition between social woman and his model of natural woman (*femme naturelle*). He leaves us in no doubt as to his assumptions: the natural state of human beings is closely tied to an animalistic way of life. He assumes that instinctive behavior determines the lives of human beings and animals in equal measure. Biological function becomes existential interpretation:

To preserve and to reproduce, these are the laws to which nature submits women. Thus to provide her own food, to accept the approaches of the male, to nourish the child that results, and not to leave it until it is capable of living without her care, these are the natural impulses women receive. Our institutions frequently take women away from them, but nature never fails to punish them for it.[8]

The portrayal of *femme naturelle* follows the division, adopted by Buffon, of each individual's life history into phases : "childhood, puberty, manhood, old age and death."[9] As a child she enjoys her mother's undivided attention. Nursed at her breast, rather than at that of a wet-nurse, she never leaves her side. Laclos' portrayal of childhood is an emphatic reaction to the era's common criticisms of infant care. His alternative conception makes clear once again his borrowings from the animal kingdom:

Whosoever desires to know the strength and delights of the sentiment of maternal love should not seek it in the palaces of the great, where self-interest and vanity alone prompt reproduction, and should avoid the huts of the poor, where misery sometimes stifles it. . . . [H]e should avoid the depraved men of our day, but consult the animals. . . . Is there any so timid that it does not become courageous in the defense of its young? any so cruel that it is not gentle and playful with them? any so fickle that it cannot concentrate on caring for them? Only woman consents to be separated from her son. . . . But no, even in her case nature was raped, not seduced. Sensitive mothers, answer me, who among you has had her newborn taken away without bathing it in a few tears?[10]

Until puberty, Laclos does not differentiate between the development of boys and girls. He views puberty as a purely instinctive development. In contrast to *femme sociale, femme naturelle* does not mature before her time, since nature is not called up by erotic fantasies, which are only a product of the state of society.[11]

The complete harmony of wants, and the possibility of satisfying them, is characteristic of woman in the state of nature and marks this epoch's superiority to the state of society. Here he conceives both of needs as purely bodily and of their satisfaction as an exclusively biological-physiological process. By refusing (in contrast to Rousseau) to take into account what differentiates human beings from animals, Laclos views the state of society as human beings' disastrous alienation from their animal roots. He asserts that human beings possess instincts akin to those of animals, and that their only chance for survival is to follow them. The maternal instinct is women's most powerful one and thus the degree of its development the measure of a woman's "naturalness." The lament about the estrangement of *femme sociale* from her primitive nature is always a lament about all the instincts, particularly the maternal instinct, that had become buried under social institutions.

Laclos simplifies Rousseau's depravation thesis by reducing his criticism of a particular form of society to the rejection of all that is social, believing that the standards for human existence can only be sought in the nonsocial, that is, the biological as a radical absolute.[12]

What would a nondepraved woman in the state of society look like, though? Laclos' notions are less concrete than Rousseau's. His construction of *femme naturelle* produces a model of womanhood that remains schematic:[13]

> Let us create at our pleasure a perfectly happy woman, as far as humanity allows it; she will be one who, born of an affectionate mother, will not be delivered as an infant into the care of a hireling; who, grown older, will be raised under the eyes of a governess who is lenient, wise and enlightened in equal measures and who, without ever using force, or boring her with her lessons, will have imparted to her all useful knowledge and kept her free of all prejudice; who, when she has reached the age of pleasure, will have found as a husband a man who always behaves like a new lover, without being jealous, who is assiduous without being importunate; who, a mother in her turn, will have tasted the sweetness of maternal love, without its perpetual worries, so frequently followed by a terrible despair; whose wise imagination will view without regret the departure of her happy youth.[14]

Laclos' redefinition of female nature is not as differentiated as that undertaken by Rousseau in *Emile* and *La Nouvelle Héloïse*. I believe that the reasons must be sought in his imprecise reading of Rousseau's theory of history. Following a typical misunderstanding, he interprets it as meaning that the epoch when animalistic individuals lived in isolation was the state appropriate to human nature. While in Rousseau the reference to woman's nature proves to be a meditation on the values of the golden age (i.e., the first *social* state), Laclos apparently understands "back to nature" in a more obvious and superficial sense. This does not prepare the ground for a more positive social role for woman. When Laclos constructs his model of *femme naturelle* as parallel to the female of the animal kingdom, he departs from Rousseau. In the First Discourse Rousseau expressly refers to human nature's independence from instinct. Thus, Jürgen von Stackelberg is not entirely correct when he writes:

Laclos' treatise represents a supplement to Rousseau's social theory, in the sense of a corrective as well as a complement. After all, in *Emile*, the misogynist Jean-Jacques' educational program, woman was largely excluded from his grand call for equality. Laclos compensated women, so to speak, for the wrongs done to them by Rousseau, who left them nothing but the role of the little housewife. . . .[15]

Even if Rousseau does not explicitly mention *femme naturelle*, his works reveal very differentiated notions of woman's nature. Laclos only points to the lacuna in Rousseau's system; he does not fill it, for his assertion that the history of woman is a history of oppression does not shape the methodology of his portrayal. This becomes clear in those passages in which he attempts to transfer *femme naturelle* (i.e., the nonenslaved woman) to the state of society. Here his portrait never progresses beyond a general argument for life outside the salons. It remains within the framework of the usual topoi marking the propagation of female sex-specific character and dispenses with the categories of emancipation and equality altogether.

The interpretation of Laclos as a feminist author, undertaken, using different arguments, by both von Stackelberg and Jaton,[16] does not seem justified. Stackelberg sees Laclos' simple observation of sexual inequality as evidence that he championed women's rights. The figure of the Marquise de Merteuil, "born to avenge her sex," appears to him a "championne du féminisme."[17] Here he fails to recognize the target of Laclos' critique. In both *Les Liaisons dangereuses* and *Des femmes et de leur éducation*, Laclos is primarily concerned not with liberating women from patriarchal chains but with demonstrating the general decay afflicting society. Woman is the chief victim of this development, which is the specific and interesting thing about Laclos' thesis. He formulates the fact that woman is oppressed by man without making excuses. Woman's character, which he historicizes, bears the marks of social depravation more clearly than man's. As a slave (of man), all the vices of the human race are redoubled in woman. She is not merely a deceiver, like a man, she is the deceiver of the deceiver. The Marquise de Merteuil is the literary embodiment of this vision. But for Laclos, restoring woman to her "true nature" no longer has a social dimension. It is reduced to a trivial set of rules for behavior. For example, woman is advised not to stay up all night, drink alcohol, or expose herself directly to the sun's rays, to bathe in cold water daily, and never to yield fully to her moods. Such advice appears motivated more by man's interest in protecting his right to pleasure than by any desire to change the course of history:

Above all, do not imitate those women, more vain than sensitive, who, content with a fleeting triumph, think only of their audience and forget their lovers; unjust women, you complain that they soon abandon you, you accuse them of thoughtlessness; seek the reason for this apparent faithlessness in yourselves; your fresh smiling face fooled them, your withered body disillusioned them. The face attracts, but it is the body that holds them. One is the net, the other the cage; but the prudent bird catcher considers the means of keeping his possible prey before setting the traps. Imitate him in his precautions, then you can worry about beautifying your face.[18]

The image of woman as a circumspect bird catcher, one that scarcely serves "woman's cause," is merely a continuation by other means of the very enslavement of woman Laclos laments. It is thus not surprising that the very superficial program of reading he develops in the third essay for a young person "with wit and a pretty face, whose rank and means put her in a position to live in the company of the most distinguished, and even to hold influence over them"[19] closes with a vista of female self-effacement: "At the same time we hope that she will acquire [from her reading] the good sense never to reveal her knowledge except to her closest friends, in confidence, so to speak. Finally, we would like to warn her that, in situations of social rivalry, in order to win the indulgence of others, the higher her reputation, the more she will need to show simplicity."[20] Jaton's euphoria at Laclos' representation, at the end of the century, of a tendency "that considers woman in her difference, without confining her to it" requires strong qualification. The "demystification of birth and of woman's physical weakness" by no means implies woman's promotion to the status of an independent and mature individual, able to live in social equality with man. As I have shown earlier for the *Encyclopédie* and Diderot's texts, this "demystification" by no means ran "counter to prevailing ideology," as Jaton claims,[21] but was, on the contrary, typical of eighteenth-century theories of femininity and the virtual precondition for the "confinement" of woman to her sexuality.

Laclos does not succeed in developing a positive alternative model out of his critique of *femme sociale*. He gives literary form only to the denatured woman at the height of social decay, in the figure of the Marquise de Merteuil. What function the feminine would serve in his ideal society remains unclear; what evidence he does provide is limited primarily to a stereotypical repetition of the call for more mother love so typical of Enlightenment discourse.

7

Female Sensibility

In the end, it was Rousseau's concept of the moral sex that came to set the terms for the late-Enlightenment *querelle des femmes*. Almost all texts on woman written in Rousseau's wake testify to the broad dissemination of *Emile* and *La Nouvelle Héloïse* in the second half of the eighteenth century. The striking effect this image of woman had cannot be explained solely by social historical arguments, let alone reduced to a patriarchal power game. Rather, Rousseau's model succeeded in responding to particular deficiencies of the nascent new society. In a world increasingly organized along utilitarian principles, the persistence of compassion became more problematic. It is precisely this aspect that contemporary "popular" texts on the woman question took up. Discussions of woman's sensibility replaced the rationalist debates about her intellect. I would like to begin in this context by returning to Thomas, whose *Essai* is typical of the reception of Rousseau's image of woman by an "enlightened" public.

Rousseau for Everywoman:
The Dual Nature of the Passions

After comparing the intellects of the sexes, Thomas contrasts their virtues.[1] Woman is at an advantage here. Thomas begins by using the assessment, frequently repeated in the literature, that women have always been more religious than men, to prove their moral superiority to the other sex. His explanation for this phenomenon rests, on the one hand, on the same sensualist epistemology that he had already used to qualify women's capacity for rational reflection. The greater sensitivity of their sensory organs, he argues, renders women more receptive to religious ritual. His second, weightier, argument is based on women's passionate nature: "[E]xtreme in their desires, nothing moderate can satisfy them."[2] To live out these desires on earth would be a crime, thus women direct their feelings and desires to another world:

> [T]hey bring to God a feeling struggling for expression, which elsewhere would be a crime. Eager for happiness, and finding little around themselves, they fling themselves into another life, towards a different world. . . . Finding themselves everywhere thwarted, prevented by the constraints of their sex from pouring out their hearts to men, and by an eternal rivalry from pouring out their hearts to women, they at least speak of their pleasures and sorrows to the Most High, who watches them, and they often confide in him their dearest weaknesses, of which nobody else is aware. Then they recall their small misdemeanors and enjoy their emotions without reproach; and, sensitive without remorse, because under the watchful eye of God, they find secret joys even in the pangs of conscience and the struggle with themselves.[3]

Thomas formulates here in theoretical terms what Diderot expresses in fictional form in *La Religieuse*: Woman's religiosity compensates for emotions and passions that would otherwise remain unexpressed. While Diderot, however, points to, or invokes, the dangers of this sublimation, female religiosity serves Thomas as an exemplary model of "ordered passionateness." This model symbolizes the very principle of female virtuousness. Consisting of that unstable equilibrium of natural, animalistic sensuality, on the one hand, and of the sense of moral norms that reins it in, on the other, it represents an equilibrium that predestines women for heroic moral achievements. If women's greater passion in love makes them capable of selfless compassionate acts, this same instinctive passion, unguided by reason, can also turn into destructive madness. To prevent this is the task of an internalized value system. While for Diderot the moral norms of female nature were purely external ones, and women remained in fact true "savages," Thomas adopts Rousseau's notion of a regulative imposed by female nature itself: modesty. "In order to preserve women's morals, attentive nature has taken care to surround them with the most gentle barriers. It has made vice more painful for them and fidelity more touching."[4] Woman is by nature more passionate in love, but she also suppresses her feelings more thoroughly than man when marital fidelity requires it. She is more capable than man "because of modesty, which even rejects that which it desires, and disputes the tenderest rights of love."[5] It is not woman who ruins society, but society woman, Thomas concludes. The breakdown of families—the root of all social decay—cannot be blamed on female nature. Woman only lives out her passions for the common good, through her love for her children, her piety, and her marital fidelity.

This assessment of Thomas' attitude, however, should not lead us to conclude that he pits the female capacity to love, as a positive principle, against rational masculine calculation. His postulate of female passion also implies the possibility of licentiousness, of the uncontrollable, which requires constant suppression. A moral corrective is necessary. Thomas, like Rousseau, accords morality a particular function for woman, that of regulating female sexuality and sensuality to ensure that biological reproduction continues along orderly lines. This form of morality implies, to be sure, a specific social context, whether that of advanced civil society or that of a state of nature, which is itself not free of projections. It relates directly, however, to woman as a natural being. Society merely functions as a mediatory social norm in order to regulate the natural process of producing offspring.

Morality has another, directly social function in Thomas's theory, though. It serves to regulate not only woman's natural carnality but also society as a whole. It serves not only the reproduction of the biological species but also the stabilization of community. Woman is accorded a specific function here; she represents something lacking in civil society. Society needs direct and spontaneous human compassion to buffer the consequences of competition.

These two functions are interdependent. It is precisely her natural instinct that renders woman eminently suited to the fulfillment of her social functions. Thomas expressly emphasizes the close connection between unconditional passion and spontaneous, compassionate behavior:

> Where is this character, at once touching and sublime, which is capable only of deep feeling? Do we find it in the cold indifference and unhappy strictness of so many fathers? No: we find it in the burning, passionate souls of mothers. It is they who, with a gesture as prompt as it is involuntary, cast themselves into the flood to pull out their child who has just carelessly fallen in. It is they who leap into the flames to grab from the fire their child sleeping in its cradle. It is they who, pale and dishevelled, rapturously hold in their arms the body of their dead son, pressing their lips to his icy ones, trying to warm with their tears his lifeless ashes. These grand gestures, these heart-

rending qualities that cause us to tremble at once with admiration, terror and tenderness, have never been, and will never be, the province of anyone but women. At such moments they possess something ineffable that raises them above everything, that seems to offer us new weapons and pushes back the known frontiers of nature.[6]

The author, as a representative of his sex, is both admiring of and terrified by these eruptions of female natural power. Spontaneous compassion can no longer be explained "rationally." It breaks the boundaries of the enlightened worldview, "the known frontiers of nature." Thomas' reaction indicates the paradox of this concept of femininity. On the one hand, mothers' spontaneous compassion requires a "burning, passionate soul"; without this temperament, all that remains is the "cold indifference and unhappy strictness" of fathers. On the other hand, it is precisely this passionate devotion that borders on madness—a madness whose outbreaks continually fire the male imagination and require constant control. It is precisely this conflict that Diderot was able to address in his review of this essay, only to resolve it one-sidedly in his model of "savage woman." Here Diderot points in a different direction from Rousseau and Rousseau's follower, Thomas. The latter attempts to handle this paradox by invoking woman's natural modesty, which continually transforms female instinct into social emotions.

Underlying the construction of controlled passion is the recognition that female closeness to nature fulfills a social function. When, in his comparison of the virtues, Thomas passes over to the social virtues, he defines them as "all tender and gentle passions."[7] According to Thomas, human coexistence is regulated, in the final analysis, by the passions. He names friendship and love as the most important here. While Thomas assumes woman's greater capacity for love to be general consensus, he asks, in his fictional dispute with Montaigne, which of the sexes is more capable of friendship. Man, Thomas asserts, does not need friendship as much as woman, who is weaker and more susceptible to the storms of life. While man is always aware of his own strength, woman is at the mercy of her feelings, and thus of her fellow human beings:

Women, in a word, for whom things are nothing and people virtually everything; women in whom everything awakens a sentiment, for whom indifference is an artificial state, & who know only how to love or to hate, would seem to feel much more vividly the freedom & the pleasure of a secret transaction, & the sweet confidences that friendship bestows and receives.[8]

Men, who belong more to the world of things, are less dependent on human relationships than women. The latter experience their environment through their feelings for others, which are always extreme ones. Composure is foreign to their nature. Montaigne objects that one must judge women not according to their nature but according to their social surroundings, particularly their way of life in the large towns; after all, the frivolous life has long since stifled female sensitivity. Women no longer express their true feelings: "[W]hat is a friendship that is always on its guard, wherein all sentiments are partially veiled, & where there is almost always a barrier between souls?"[9] True friendship requires a stable character, one that shrinks neither from sacrifice nor danger. Women's inconstancy, as well as their passive existence, are hindrances, for only grand interests unify friends: "[W]ithout grand interests one never develops a close bond. And women by their very condition are dedicated to repose."[10]

In his dialogue, Thomas sketches two different types of friendship. The idea of male friendship, attributed to Montaigne, was based on "grand interests." This kind of friendship is "imposing and severe: in order to fulfill its duties well, one must be able to speak and understand the manly and austere language of truth."[11] For this reason, so he concludes from the fictive dispute with his intellectual forefather, one should choose a male friend for "important occasions." But Thomas senses, more vaguely than reflectively, that those very interest-based male friendships, which two hundred years earlier had held out to Montaigne the promise of emotional fulfillment, were not without their shortcomings. "Generally speaking, men possess the outward forms of friendship more than its graces, and their tenderest sentiments do not extend to the little things that mean so very much."[12] Woman, though, knows how to smooth the ripples that occur in men's dealings with each other. While men are guided by such feelings as ambition, pride, and the desire for possessions, which they hide behind such lofty concepts as patriotism, women concentrate completely on the individual human being. "Everything disposes them to the sentiment of pity. Their more delicate sensibilities rebel against injuries and pain. . . . What woman has ever failed to respect misfortune."[13] Without women's spontaneous compassion, the social fabric would disintegrate. Women possess virtues, such as gentleness (*douceur*), the art of looking past the weaknesses of others, of not hurting others, the complaisance to accept unfamiliar ideas: in short, virtues indispensable in daily life. "They [women's virtues] are to ordinary life what ready money is to commerce."[14] Feminine compassion compensates for the damage done by calculating masculine rationality: "[G]enerally speaking, one may say that women correct that which an excess of passions has made a bit hard in commerce among men. Their delicate hand softens, so to speak, and polishes society's springs."[15] Thus Thomas' advice leads to a synthesis between his own position and Montaigne's. "For great occasions one should wish for a man friend, but for the happiness of everyday life, the friendship of a woman."[16] Everyday happiness was no longer in the power of men. Thomas blames this on men's emotional structure: He takes patriotism as paradigmatic of the male inclination toward abstract emotions:

> I have no intention of denigrating patriotism. It is the most generous of sentiments; at least it is the one that has produced the most great men, and that gave birth to those ancient heroes whose history daily astounds our imagination and reproaches our weakness. But if we wish to dissect these motive forces, and examine their composition at close range, we will find that patriotism in men is almost always a mixture of pride, self-interest, property, hope, the memory of actions performed or sacrifices made on behalf of fellow citizens, and a certain artificial enthusiasm that strips them of themselves, in order to transfer their entire existence to the body of the state.[17]

Women, in contrast, have never had the opportunity to sacrifice their lives for the state. Hence they have been "less altered than we [men] by the social institutions in which they take less part." For this reason they love their own families more than the state. "A single human being means more to them than a nation, and one day when they are alive more than twenty centuries they will never experience."[18]

The division of emotions into inner and outer worlds, and their gender-specific distribution, runs through Thomas' balancing of masculine and feminine virtues. He establishes their attributions, if not with the same programmatic thoroughness as Rousseau, placing spontaneous compassion, family, and nature on the one side, and abstract humaneness, the state/public, and divergence from nature on the other. This split correlates to the dichotomy between masculine rationality and feminine sensibility. Since woman, as a result of her physical constitution, has more capacity for emotion and less for reason she is, according to Thomas, in a better position than man to fulfill the universal function of social intermediary. The necessary moral feeling, after all, has its roots in unadulterated, unreflected nature.

The perception of the insufficiency of human interaction in a society of competing individuals leads to a division of the emotions into social, abstract feelings on the one hand and direct, private ones on the other. Their gender-specific assignment—which the prevailing division of labor renders plausible—does not fully account for the particular nature attributed to the female human being. An "ideological residue" remains, consisting of the conception of the different characters of man and woman not simply as *differences*, but as mutually exclusive *oppositions*. It is conceivable, for example, that familial morality, for which woman is responsible, could also require rational thought. Evidently, though, the opposite is the case. Woman can fulfill her moral function only by avoiding rational reflection. That, at least, is what is suggested by the previously cited pathos-laden descriptions of mothers jumping into floods or braving flames to rescue their children and other similar examples of female selflessness presented by both Thomas and Roussel. They act not on rational understanding but on instinct. "Above all, they have that sensitivity of instinct that acts before thinking, & that is already off to the rescue while man is still deliberating."[19] Roussel wonders whether the perfection of rational thought does not destroy acts of spontaneous charity: "Might it be true, as has been said, that this precious instinct, with which nature has taken care to bind men to each other, deteriorates and weakens as reflection becomes perfected?"[20]

Thomas' view of reason as deleterious to such compassionate behavior closely follows Rousseau's theory in which rational calculating reason is conceived of as a means to achieve selfish ends. According to him, social reproduction would no longer be guaranteed if it were not, in the sphere of immediate human relations, for a morality far removed from all (competitive) rational considerations. This morality must rest on a counterauthority—immediate spontaneous feeling:

> As regards morality, everything in them [women] takes the form of sentiment: they always judge things and people by this yardstick. . . . This inclination was doubtless necessary in the sex whom nature made the depository of that part of the human race which is still weak & helpless. They would have perished a thousand times over if forced to rely on the hesitant and uncertain aid of cold reason.[21]

Conversely, the "naturalizing" of morality also leads to the "naturalizing" of the feminine. The distance between rationality and emotionality is that between the state of society and the state of nature. Femininity represents nature for two reasons: on the one hand, woman's biological constitution, her capacity for childbearing brings her closer than man to the origins of human creatureliness. On the other hand, her social role consists in preserving emotions that have not become denaturalized—a role whose anthropological justification is derived from woman's biological constitution, because compassion has its place in the familial sphere, that is, that of biological reproduction.

The Limited Scope of Female Sensibility

In Thomas' system, the gender-specific attribution of reason and emotion by no means predestines woman to act as moral authority for society as a whole, even in the age of emotion-based morality. The residues of compassion existing in the niches of bourgeois calculating rationality bear traces of woman's social limitations. Woman is permitted to attain moral greatness only in literature, if at all. In real life, her devotion to individual people often appears ridiculous. This, at least, is the impression Thomas conveys when he expressly declares woman responsible for the "little emotions" and desires to see her excluded from all truly significant matters.

Nothing escapes her keen perceptions. Always observing, woman ably recognizes and evaluates the human weaknesses of those around her. Thomas portrays her as a great psychologist who can see through human passions to their furthest ramifications. This ability, however, by no means predestines her to hold public office, in which she would have to direct others. Instead of employing her psychological insight for the common good, woman only uses this capacity for private, petty tyranny within her small sphere of influence:

> Thus in society the art of government is that of flattering characters, whereas the art of administration is almost always that of fighting them. Even the knowledge of human nature required for each is not the same. In the one, one must know the weaknesses of men, in the other their strengths. The one uses the failings for his petty ends, the other discovers the great qualities that stem from these very failings.[22]

Here Thomas attributes to woman not only rational incompetence but also deficient emotionality. In his balancing of feminine and masculine virtues, Thomas reaches the conclusion that although woman, in her devotion to individuals, surpasses man in love, tenderness, pity, and so on, she lacks the requisite capacity for abstraction for such lofty emotions as "patriotism" (*amour de la patrie*) or "love of humanity" (*amour de l'humanité*), or for "austere and impartial justice" (*justice austère et impartiale*). Thus she is also lacking in the "political or moral spirit that governs."

Through his attempt to set up a hierarchy of sentiment—and to relegate woman to its lower levels—Thomas is able to extend women's cultural incompetence to spheres for which they might appear, because of their greater emotionality, to be better suited than men. While Mme de Lambert, for example, still emphasized women's supposedly greater sensitivity in order to attribute to them a particular talent for the arts, Thomas endeavors to show that women's great capacity for imagination is not enough to make artists of them. In explanation, he cites woman's passive way of life, which shields her from extreme emotions:

> Man, always active, is exposed to storms. The Poet's imagination feeds on the mountain peaks, at the edge of volcanoes, on the seas, on the battlefield, or in the midst of ruins; & he never feels voluptuous and tender ideas more strongly than after being shaken by great upheavals. But are women, with their soft, sedentary lives, experiencing less the contrast between the pleasant and the terrible, as capable of feeling and describing even pleasant things as those thrown into the most contrary situations, who pass quickly from one emotion to the next?[23]

If Thomas makes a correct observation here, that is, that participation in the whole of life is a necessary precondition for artistic creativity, he does not consider this the primary reason for women's underrepresentation in the arts. Even before external circumstances intervene, female nature itself prevents artistic creation. "I wonder whether their more delicate fibers might not fear strong sensations that exhaust them, seeking instead gentle, restful ones."[24] Woman's physical constitution prohibits direct contact with reality. Being a woman becomes a "protected occupation" (Virginia Woolf's *A Room of One's Own*), whose natural boundaries run along the threshhold of stormy daily life. Vivid female imagination is thus not creative and active, or productive, but at best contemplative. Woman's easily overstrained nerves permit no direct contact with life; they can only endure it by reflecting it. "Perhaps their imagination, though lively, resembles a mirror that reflects everything but creates nothing."[25] Only in reflections do they experience passions, which are never truly their own—with one exception: love. But even the experience of love has its limits, for because of their different natures only man lives out his emotions while women, "obliged by duty, by the reserve of their sex, by the wish for a certain gracefulness that softens everything," suppress and, finally, weaken them: "A passing constraint fires the passions; a lasting constraint deadens or extinguishes them."[26] The capacity to reflect the feelings of others thus prevents active experience and limits woman to a passive "surrender to emotions." This inability to create something out of themselves is also the reason for their incapacity for artistic creativity. The contradictions inherent in Thomas's theory are obvious. If the proof of women's intellectual inferiority on the grounds of their purported hypersensitivity at least had some "logical" consistency, that of their artistic incapacity was patently absurd. After all, when it came to demonstrating their tendency toward superstition, women's imaginative powers were considered vivid, even magically potent, but then they were to be reduced to dull mediocrity. With the fall of the ideal of the learned woman, which had been closely tied to rationalist epistemology, more was lost than the demand for equal educational opportunities. Exclusion from the society of thinkers also cut the "woman of sensibility" down to size, conceding to her only "sensitivity in detail" (*sensibilité du détail*).[27]

Raising Girls to Be Society's Moral Conscience: Women's Pedagogical Writings

The distribution of sentimental and intellectual education between the two sexes and the demand for women's moral education are also reflected in the pedagogical writings that, particularly from mid-century on, often appeared in quite large editions. Frequently penned by female authors, they reflect the tensions experienced by women trying to emancipate themselves. Enlightenment educational aspirations were one of the factors leading many women to demand their right to knowledge. Efforts to establish *female* education, however, also represented a step in the direction of gender-specific training. The rationalist egalitarian postulate of sexless intellect gave way to the notion of a sex-specific character reflected in every aspect of human life. Educating girls increasingly came to mean training them to be the moral sex. The acquisition of knowledge, only recently accepted as a general female right, was immediately placed in the service of this aim. Knowledge was to be neither an end in itself nor part of preparation for a profession.

Professionalism was considered virtually an abuse of female education. Mme de Miremont, who developed an extensive twelve-volume curriculum for girls that conveyed an outline of Abbé Nollet's experimental physics and an overview of French history as well as a multitude of practical and theoretical information, expressly emphasizes the limits of her thirst for knowledge: "We are agreed here on the uselessness of the exact sciences for Women; but what study is better suited to training the mind for accuracy than that segment of Physics resting upon experiment? The brevity of these sections will show, nevertheless, that I am not teaching my sex to be so arrogant as to lay claim to everything."[28] In her own work, Miremont allows herself to be guided by just this female nonprofessionalism: "The art of teaching Women includes the talent of pleasing them. Let us go further: the art of persuasion is nothing for them, if one does not hold their interest. In order to capture their minds, one must speak to their *hearts*" [emphasis added].[29] She justifies her own role as author by the express approval of her husband, who appended a two-page "Notice" to her *Prospectus*:

> Her ideas on the inadequacies of present Education seemed to me so correct, and the methods she daily employs to remedy them so simple & so well organized, that I encouraged her to undertake this work. It was by no means the vanity to appear as an author that moved her, but a much rarer motive, her desire to oblige her husband, & perhaps also to set up a plan confirming her method.[30]

Baron H. de L., who wished to remain anonymous because he feared ridicule for his connection to a wife who was an "author and wit" (*auteur et bel esprit*), also gives us to understand that the work in question was not that of his wife alone: "I like to think that she had need of my experience; that she enjoyed having recourse to my knowledge; bound by matrimony, and even more closely united by sentiment, this Work is that of two happy creatures who communicated their souls & their thoughts: the child of happiness, I hope it will prosper."[31] Even as a published author, Mme de Miremont does not depart from the role of a woman requiring male support.

Mme Espinassy, whose *Essai sur l'éducation des Demoiselles* (Essay on the Education of Young Ladies) offers mothers principles for the upbringing of their daughters, also expressly emphasizes that even the study of physics, which she recommends, is not intended to turn daughters into learned ladies. "The sciences . . . will be more a diversion for your daughter than a serious subject of study."[32] For Espinassy, whose addressees are the women of high society, diversions for empty days are a moral concern. It is boredom that pushes a young girl to marry "before her time." This "dangerous" period between girls' awakening "taste for the pleasures of society" and marriageable age must be bridged with activities that divert the premature desire for a romantic attachment. For this reason, she warns against reading novels, which she would like to see strictly forbidden to girls under the age of eighteen. Novels glorify love so unduly that the unwitting reader's only wish is "to put into practice the lessons provided by her reading." For this reason Espinassy, who anticipated the dangers of Bovarysm a hundred years before Flaubert, recommends fairy tales as reading matter. In them the fantastic (*merveilleux*) is always recognizable as fiction, thus removing the danger that girls might take it for reality. She firmly rejects any higher degree of realism; "the more plausible the novel, the more dangerous it is."[33]

Despite the all-powerful influence of Rousseau's educational ideals, though, debates about woman's social position continued. Even if broad consensus existed that educating women meant educating their moral sentiments, there was no agreement as to the extent of these supposedly female sentiments. The reduction of female feeling to the "little emotions" as undertaken by Thomas was rejected particularly by those women concerned, out of Enlightenment motives, with girls' education. The question of educating girls as moral beings, which Espinassy's work handles rather mildly in the form of warnings against pubescent daydreaming and enthusiasm, and limits to the domestication of woman as sexual being, takes on a social dimension in Mme de Miremont, which also goes beyond the scope of Thomas' theories. She attributes the lamentable general moral decay and lacking grandeur of her age to its neglect of girls' education.

In classical antiquity, an epoch that serves as her model, women were respected as "the guarantors and preservers of the virtues."[34] Her own age cut a very poor figure in comparison. Men, "those arbiters of the universe,"[35] had reduced women to the playthings of their passions, requiring of them only so much virtue as they needed "to make their pleasures as agreeable as possible."[36] In corrupting women, however, men had succeeded in harming themselves. It was, after all, women who—as those responsible for raising the next generation—determined the rise or fall of entire societies. She qualifies the optimistic belief in the Enlightenment's moral efficacy. "Men seek to improve themselves as they become enlightened. The sciences act upon the mind, and the mind in turn moves the heart,"[37] she asserts in accordance with Enlightenment notions of education. But, she concedes, man's encyclopedic accumulation of knowledge remains inefficacious so long as no educational program is established for women that promotes their natural inclination toward virtue. Miremont, whose model is not civil society but Greek and early Roman society, still believes in the identity of public and private virtue. As is appropriate to her lofty vision of a society whose members prize the honor of their country more than their own lives, she assigns great importance to the protectress of morality. Woman is responsible not only for family morality, as she is, for example, in Thomas' writings. She also places her person in the service of the state, just as man does. Miremont's portrait of the valiant man (*homme brave*), who prefers glory to life, has its counterpart in her model of the "wise woman" (*femme sage*), who, when required, overcomes maternal feelings in order to fulfill her duty toward society. "In those days [ancient Greece and Rome] one heard more than one Spartan ask not 'is my son alive' but 'were we victorious?' . . . At that time woman cared for the well-being of her homeland, she was interested in its glory."[38] These remarks are directed not only at the ladies of Parisian high society, but also against the bourgeois notions of "wife and mother," and particularly against "Monsieur Rousseau, who belongs to those famous men whose errors one would sooner see forgotten."[39] Even if Miremont agrees with him that woman is a moral authority, she vehemently rejects the reduction of her moral responsibility to the sphere of childraising, and of her moral feelings to spontaneous instinct. She pointedly places woman's sense of honor above mother love, although in another context she argues emphatically—in contrast to aristocratic practice—for close contact between children and their own mothers.

While Thomas still expressly declared mother love and patriotism to be two antagonistic emotions, and denied women the abstract virtues, Miremont takes up the tradition of Poulain de la Barre to the extent that she rejects the hierarchy of emotions set up by Enlightenment thinkers and does not attribute female moral sentiment to ostensibly biological-physiological causes, regarding it instead as the result of wisdom (*sagesse*) acquired through education. Woman's moral action is thus just as influenced by rational considerations as man's code of honor. Poulain de la

Barre's famous dictum, transformed to read 'virtue has no sex' would be a fitting motto for Miremont's reflections.

In the second half of the eighteenth century, the *querelle des femmes* was transferred to the plane of debates on the moral authority of the two sexes. The existence of sex-specific character was no longer seriously doubted. The question of woman's part in the progress of the human intellect had been answered in the negative. All that remained open was the social scope of her emotions.

The "secret" opposition to female self-effacement is also expressed by Louise d'Epinay, whose *Conversations d'Emilie* (Conversations with Emilie) was one of the period's best-known pedagogical works. She refuses to accept that "persons belonging to our sex should have limits set upon their knowledge"[40] and compiles a precise program of education for her niece Emilie, who, unlike Rousseau's Sophie, is not to be kept in perfect ignorance, but introduced as early as possible to the educational products of the male world. The times when knowledge was explicitly claimed for women, as Caffiaux or Puisieux did, were however over before they really began. In her biography, Elisabeth Badinter shows how d'Epinay stoically mastered her resignation at the impossibility of putting her goals into practice. "Rather than struggle with a society closed to women in order to gain access to the domains reserved for men, Mme d'Epinay preferred to give Emilie the weapons for inner independence."[41] These were the weapons of stoic morality, the sacrifice of outer happiness to inner contentment. Like the Marquise de Lambert fifty years earlier, if for different reasons, d'Epinay seeks refuge in the quiet sense of inner happiness. "One may enjoy all external advantages, great riches, good health, but still not be happy, for true happiness depends upon ourselves."[42] The postulate of intellectual equality between man and woman does not lead her to demand social equality. D'Epinay attempts to preserve the learned woman within the Enlightenment ideal of the mother, making the inculcation of scholarly abilities part of her educational practice and calling for "quiet learning." But even this defensive type of self-assertion met with little success. D'Epinay may have won an academy competition against her opponent, Genlis, a follower of Rousseau, with her *Conversations* in 1775, but it was Rousseau's image of woman that spoke to the spirit of the age and molded girls' education. "Created to run a household, to raise children, to depend upon a master who will demand now their advice, now their obedience, women must thus be orderly, patient, prudent, fair and sound of mind. . . ."[43]

It is doubtless no accident that Diderot published his critique of Thomas' *Essai* while Mme d'Epinay, despite the encouragement of her close friend the abbé Galiani, held back her own. In contrast to Diderot, who accused Thomas of not making enough distinctions between the characters of the two sexes, an outraged d'Epinay wrote to Galiani after reading the *Essai*, "Men and women, sharing the same nature and constitution, are subject to the same defects, the same virtues and the same vices."[44] Her egalitarianism contradicted the "knowledge" of her age. The model of sexless reason, with all its implications for the image of woman, could no longer hold out against the theories presented by contemporary anthropology, moral philosophy, or philosophy of history.

Conclusion

Nature was the central concept of the eighteenth century.[1] *Human* nature, in particular, became the age's most important object of study. I have tried to show that the definition of human nature was not always congruent with that of female nature. Although the texts I treat do not lend themselves to concluding generalizations, marking as they do individual stages rather than a continuous development, a trend does emerge: In the eighteenth century, gender difference was infused with a new and thoroughgoing anthropological depth. In the period I studied woman was not merely subjected to strict norms; her very nature was accorded a precisely defined place in the anthropological system. Out of this process arose the paradox that the very concept of nature, which when applied to the human individual signified emancipation, was enlisted to exclude woman from this emancipation.

The theories with whose aid this occurred cannot be understood as purely "ideological," in the sense of interest-based. Their argumentative strategies cannot be explained by simple reference to a patriarchal will to power. Even if the bare fact of the existence of patriarchal conditions (not only) during this period is uncontroversial, it would be too easy to regard the intention to preserve them as a determining objective, from which perspective all facets of the representation of female existence could be explained. Feminist scholarship does not always succeed in avoiding this pitfall. Actual repression, and its legitimation, have all too often become the central hypotheses in studies of discourses on woman.[2] This, in my opinion, shortsighted perspective leaves the impression that theories of female nature were expressly "invented" with evil intent to discriminate against women.

I have attempted to circumvent this approach (which seems to me in essence a purely moralistic critique) by analyzing the discourses on women in conjunction with the *scientific* discourses of the period. However misogynist they may have been, one cannot deny that Enlightenment authors approached their "subject" with scholarly intentions. If we reject this assumption, their conceptions do indeed appear arbitrary. But precisely those arguments employed within a scientific discourse are anything but random. They exist in a necessary relation to that discourse, and it is here that our own scholarly interest today begins.

It became evident that significant theorems which passed into the *querelle des femmes* were already available, in a partially elaborated form, in certain contemporary disciplines (biology, medicine) and in the history of philosophy (anthropology, philosophy of history, moral philosophy, epistemology). On the one hand, these theoretical "preliminary studies" or models of argumentation determined the *form* assumed by the specific discourse in the Enlightenment debates on woman. On the other hand, however—and this is surely more controversial—I have tried to demonstrate that the individual disciplines and philosophical elements of theory employed were also decisive in determining the *direction* of argumentation within the discourse.

The substance with which the concept "woman's nature" was filled, its potentials and limits, was only partially determined by patriarchal power structures. The elimination of the ideal of the learned woman is characteristic. The fact that in the "age of reason" woman's capacity for abstract thought was disputed with radical thoroughness did not result from men's desire to keep her stupid so that he might rule her more easily. Her exclusion from the social process of labor also only provides a limited answer. Far more decisive is the fact that, at the very moment when society put its trust in the power of reason, reason was quickly coming to smack of utilitarianism, egoism, coldness, calculation, and inhumanity.[3] The very valorization of reason helped reveal its deficiencies under certain social conditions. Adherents of the Enlightenment realized that the rationality of commerce could not be readily transferred to the sphere of interpersonal relations. This explains the calls for morality—but for a private morality, subject to its own laws, additional to and separate from the public sphere. Private morality depended not on selfish, calculating reason, but rather on *sentiment naturel*.

This shift of emphasis from a morality based on reason to one based on sentiment[4] is a phenomenon at first glance quite unconnected to the woman question. It was, rather, a general phenomenon that accompanied the fears aroused by bourgeois modes of doing business and theoretical reflections about this situation. This new emphasis is interesting for our analysis insofar as it deeply influenced definitions of the feminine. Morality based on sentiment did not, after all, dispense with the functions of reason. In Enlightenment moral philosophy, both elements—instinctive, spontaneous moral feeling and the rational weighing of interests—were necessary for moral action. But the shift of emphasis from reason to sentiment was extended to women. The contradictory relations between calculating reason and compassionate feeling, between private and public morality, were borne unequally by men and women. The greater emphasis on "natural foundations"—only one tendency in the anthropological discourse of the time—is magnified in the case of women. Women become the "moral sex." It was not a matter of discriminating against one sex, but rather of distributing objective functions, that is, of allocating each its place in the theoretical system. The main problem was not which radius of action the male sex should allot the female but how rational a society could be or, rather, which type of reason was effective enough in the area of interpersonal relations to keep the whole system functioning.

The discussion surrounding woman's moral responsibility is by no means a thing of the past. Through its demands for political and social rights, the new women's movement of the 1970s and 1980s reopened the debate. The "relationship work" which women had previously been doing unnoticed was brought to public attention, not least because this work is frequently no longer performed by women. Conservative warnings about the "masculinization" of women have their counterpart in the decided valorization of female sex-specific character and demands for its social recognition by segments of the women's movement. Neither position is merely "ideological." They reveal, first, that the norms ascribed to female nature are not identical to understandings of "human" nature and, second, that woman's move into the male world of work has created an actual vacuum, one which manifests itself not simply in sinking birth rates but, rather—and this seems to me more significant—in the loss of a part of this "nature," that is, of particular ethical norms and behaviors. "Kindness, gentleness, modesty, the readiness to make sacrifices": Women today, socially equal to men, identify as little with this canon of virtues—set up by Desmahis in the *Encyclopédie*—as most men ever did. The necessity for these virtues has nonetheless by no means disappeared.[5]

The Enlightenment's legacy is evident in the current *querelle des femmes*'s reintroduction of the question of female rationality. In contrast to the eighteenth century, nobody seriously doubts women's capacity for abstract thought anymore. Even today, though, the use of this capacity remains associated with unemotional, inhumane, and selfish calculation. The wave of "new emotionality" that peaked in the women's movement of the 1970s and 1980s, expressed in a flood of literature based on autobiographical experience, frequently enunciated a conscious rejection of objectivity, generalization, and analysis.[6] The Enlightenment discussion on women led to the denigration of learned women as "bluestockings," stamping them as outsiders. As a result, no other female social type has had to struggle so hard against accusations of prudery and emotional coldness. The new search for specifically female values and the "new femininity," set in conscious opposition to the masculine world, are only the reverse sides of precisely that Enlightenment rationality that is under attack: In other words, the former belongs to the latter. Thus the very rejection of rationality and of the "Enlightenment principle" with which (not only) segments of the women's movement have declared war on patriarchal power structures itself belongs in the Enlightenment tradition.

Notes

Introduction

1. See Renate Baader, "Die Literatur der Frau oder die Aufklärung der kleinen Schritte," in *Neues Handbuch der Literaturwissenschaft*, ed. Jürgen von Stackelberg (Wiesbaden: Athenaion, 1980), vol. 13, pp. 79–106. On the following discussion, see also my article "Vom Aufstieg und Fall der gelehrten Frau: Einige Aspekte der 'Querelle des Femmes' im XVIII. Jahrhundert," *Lendemains* 25–26 (1982), 157–67.

2. "La femme au XVIIIe siècle est le principe qui gouverne, la raison qui dirige, la voix qui commande; elle est la cause universelle et fatale, l'origine des évènements, la source des choses." Edmond and Jules de Goncourt, *La Femme au 18e siècle*, ed. Elisabeth Badinter (Paris: Flammarion, 1982), p. 291.

3. See, e.g., Vera Lee, *The Reign of Women in Eighteenth-Century France* (Cambridge, Mass.: Harvard UP, 1975).

4. Pierre Choderlos de Laclos, *Des femmes et de leur éducation*, in *Œuvres complètes*, ed. Laurent Versini (Paris: Gallimard, 1979), pp. 387–434. "La femme naturelle est, ainsi que l'homme, un être libre et puissant" (p. 393).

5. This term is a translation of the German *Geschlechtscharakter*, meaning the sum of the social, emotional, and intellectual traits attributed to male or female human beings based on their biological sex. The eighteenth-century notion of *Geschlechtscharakter* is discussed in detail in a pathbreaking essay by Karin Hausen that has exercised an enormous influence on German feminist scholarship, particularly in the field of history: "Die Polarisierung der 'Geschlechtscharaktere': Eine Spiegelung der Dissoziation von Erwerbs- und Familienleben," in *Sozialgeschichte der Familie in der Neuzeit Europas*, ed. Werner Conze (Stuttgart: Klett, 1976), pp. 363–93. English trans., "Family and Role-Division: The Polarisation of Sexual Stereotypes in the Nineteenth Century—An Aspect

of the Dissociation of Work and Family Life," trans. Cathleen Catt, in *The German Family: Essays on the Social History of the Family in Nineteenth- and Twentieth-Century Germany*, ed. Richard J. Evans and W. R. Lee (London: Croom Helm, 1981), pp. 51–83.

6. See, e.g., Edward Shorter, *The Making of the Modern Family* (New York: Basic Books, 1975); Jean-Louis Flandrin, *Families in Former Times: Kinship, Household, Sexuality* (Cambridge: Cambridge UP, 1979); and Karin Hausen, "Polarisierung."

7. See Elisabeth Badinter, *Mother Love: Myth and Reality*, trans. Roger de Garis (New York: Macmillan, 1981), particularly her chapter on "The Economic Discourse."

8. Philippe Ariès, *Centuries of Childhood: A Social History of Family Life*, trans. Robert Baldick (New York: Vintage, 1962).

9. A typical example is the French bestseller of 1983, Philippe Sollers' novel *Femmes* (Paris: Gallimard, 1983); English trans., *Women*, trans. Barbara Bray (New York: Columbia UP, 1990). The novel presents a modern variation on the Enlightenment topos of the impossibility of a rounded development of the female personality. Woman is no longer denied, as in Rousseau, the capacity to develop her intellect as fully as man: In the age of "women's lib," Sollers paints a social tableau crawling with women journalists, scholars, politicians, presidents, etc. Aside from the fact that these professional women's achievements are mediocre at best, they also achieve social and intellectual emancipation only by sacrificing their "human" qualities. What remains are crippled beings whose boundless appetite for success causes them to smother all humanitarian compassion.

10. In their *Histoire du féminisme français: Du moyen âge à nos jours* (Paris: Edition des femmes, 1977), Maïté Albistur and Daniel Armogathe speak of a "Rebondissement de la querelle des femmes."

11. For an overview of the treatises on these questions, see Jeannette Geffriaud-Rosso, "Pour une théorie de la femme: Traités et dissertations de 1600 à 1789," in her *Histoire du féminisme français aux XVIIᵉ et XVIIIᵉ siècles* (Pisa: Goliardica, 1984), pp. 163–211.

12. Virginia Woolf, *A Room of One's Own* (New York: Harçourt Brace Jovanovich, 1929), pp. 45–46.

13. The texts I use may be classified as follows: (1) theoretical writings, some in the fields of moral philosophy and anthropology (Rousseau, Laclos), some approaching the genre of the popular political pamphlet (Poulain, Thomas, Archambault, Caffiaux, Puisieux). These belong to the *querelle des femmes* proper (chapters 1, 3, 5, and 6); (2) articles from the *Encyclopédie* (chapter 2); (3) medical texts (Roussel) (chapter 3); (4) literary texts (Rousseau, Diderot) (chapters 4 and 5); and (5) pedagogical texts (Miremont, Espinassy, d'Epinay) (chapter 6).

14. Paul Hoffmann, *La Femme dans la pensée des Lumières* (Paris: Ophrys,

1977), p. 1. "Nulle causalité ni logique, ni sociologique n'explique l'évolution des idées sur la femme. L'ensemble des discours qui dessinent, à chaque moment de l'histoire, son visage éphémère et éternel, ne saurait constituer une science."
    15. Hoffmann, *La Femme*, p. 18. "C'est avouer que nous avons pris parti! Mais l'objet même de notre étude excluait l'objectivité. Nul ne peut parler de la femme, s'il ne s'engage, s'il ne se compromet."
    16. Hoffmann, *La Femme*, p. 19. "A nul moment la liberté de la femme n'apparaît plus problématique que lorsqu'elle est appelée, par sa nature même, à porter l'enfant et à le mettre au monde. Nul moment où apparaisse mieux l'empire du corps; mais nulle occasion non plus pour la raison qui soit plus propice pour montrer quels sont ses devoirs et ses pouvoirs."

Chapter 1

    1. Philippe Florent de Puisieux, *La Femme n'est pas inférieure à l'homme.* Traduit de l'anglois (London, 1750), BN Rés. R 2167; Dom Philippe-Joseph Caffiaux, *Défense du Beau Sexe, ou Memoires historiques, philosophiques et critiques pour servir d'Apologie aux femmes* (Amsterdam, 1753), 3 vols., BN R 24131–24134.
    2. Their most important writings are: Christine de Pizan, *Livre de la Cité des Dames* (1404), *The Book of the City of Ladies*, trans. Earl J. Richards (New York: Persea, 1982); *Livre des trois vertus* (1408); Marguerite de Navarre, *L'Heptameron* (1542–1543), *The Heptameron*, trans. Paul A. Chilton (Harmondsworth: Penguin, 1984); Louise Labé, *Débat de folie et de l'amour* (1555). On these issues see Dietmar Rieger, "Die französische Dichterin im Mittelalter: Marie de France—die 'trobairitz'—Christine de Pizan," in *Die Französische Autorin vom Mittelalter bis zur Gegenwart*, ed. Renate Baader and Dietmar Fricke (Wiesbaden: Athenaion, 1979), pp. 29–48; Klaus Ley, "Weibliche Lyrik der Renaissance: Pernette du Guillet und Louise Labé," *Die Französische Autorin*, pp. 49–62; Dietmar Fricke, "Wiedergeburt in Lieben und Schreiben—Weibliche erzählende Prosa der Renaissance: Jeanne Flore, Hélisanne de Crenne, Marguerite de Navarre, *Die Französische Autorin*, pp. 63–76.
    3. For two examples among many, see Jean Tixier's fourteen-volume collection, *De Memorabilibus et Claris Mulieribus aliquot diversorum scriptorum opera* (1521), and Guillaume Postel's 1553 *Les Très Merveilleuses Victoires des femmes du nouveau monde, et comme elles doivent à tout le monde, par raison, commander, et même à ceux qui auront la monarchie du monde vieil.* See also Georges Ascoli, "Les Idées féministes en France," *Revue de synthèse historique*, 13 (1906), 25–57 and 161–84, esp. 31ff.; and Ian MacLean, *Women Triumphant: Feminism in French Literature, 1610–1652* (Oxford: Clarendon, 1977). For a chronological list of all sixteenth-century published contributions to the *querelle*

des femmes, see Maïté Albistur and Daniel Armogathe, *Histoire du féminisme français*, (Paris: Edition des femmes, 1977), pp. 81ff.

4. Ascoli, "Les Idées féministes," 31ff.

5. Ibid., 32.

6. *De l'égalité des deux sexes: Discours physique et morale, où l'on voit l'importance de se défaire des Préjugez* (Paris: Jean Du Puis, 1673; rpt. Paris: Fayard, 1984), p. 9: "[N]ous sommes remplis de préjugez, et . . . il faut y renoncer absolument, pour avoir des connoissances claires et distinctes." English trans., *The Woman as Good as the Man: Or, The Equality of Both Sexes* (London, 1677). On Poulain de la Barre's Cartesianism and on the influence of other contemporary philosophers, see Madeleine Alcover's monograph, *Poulain de la Barre: Une aventure philosophique* (Paris: Papers on French Seventeenth-Century Literature, 1981). On the term *préjugé* as a central category in Poulain's thought, see Geneviève Fraisse, "Poulain de la Barre, ou le procès des préjugés," *Corpus: Revue de philosophie* 1 (May 1985), 27–42. On the sociological underpinnings of rationalist feminism, see Inge Baxmann, "Von der Egalité im Salon zur Citoyenne: Einige Aspekte der Genese des bürgerlichen Frauenbildes," in *Frauen in der Geschichte*, ed. Annette Kuhn and Jörn Rüsen (Düsseldorf: Schwann, 1983), vol. 3, pp. 109–37, and Christine Fauré, "Poulain de la Barre, sociologue et penseur," *Corpus* 1 (May 1985), 43–52.

7. René Descartes, *Discours de la méthode*, Œuvres et Lettres, ed. André Bridoux (Paris: Gallimard, 1953), p. 26. "Le bon sens est la chose du monde la mieux partagée."

8. de la Barre, *De l'égalité*, pp. 59ff.

9. Ibid., p. 59.

10. Ibid, p. 20. "[E]lles [les femmes] n'ont été assujetties que par la Loy du plus fort et . . . ce n'a pas esté faute de capacité naturelle ni de merite qu'elles n'ont point partagé avec nous ce qui élève nostre Sexe dessus du leur."

11. Avertissement, *De l'éducation des dames pour la conduite de l'esprit dans les sciences et dans les mœurs* (Paris, 1674), n.p. "[P]ar la mesme raison que les ouvrages qui se font pour les hommes servent également aux femmes, n'y ayant qu'une méthode pour instruire les uns & les autres, comme estans de mesme espece."

12. Ibid. "Or, la principale & la plus importante [maxime] de toutes est qu'il faut établir dans les hommes, autant qu'on le peut, une raison souveraine qui les rend capable de juger de toutes choses sainement & sans prévention."

13. de Puisieux, *La Femme*. Barbier substantiates Puisieux's account but does not mention the name of the English author either. Antoine Alexandre Barbier, *Dictionnaire des ouvrages anonymes et pseudonymes composés*, 4 vols. (Paris: Barrois, 1822–127), vol. 2, p. 12 (no. 6684).

14. de Puisieux, *La Femme*, p. 35.

15. Ibid., p. 83: "[I]ls [les hommes] sont si accoutumés à voir les choses telles

qu'elles sont maintenant, qu'ils ne peuvent se figurer qu'elles puissent être autrement."

16. Ibid., p. 53. "Tout le monde scait que la différence des sexes ne regarde que le corps seulement, & n'existe que dans les parties qui servent à la propagation de la nature humaine."

17. Ibid, pp. 89–112.

18. Ibid., p. 115.

19. Fernand Braudel and Ernest Labrousse, *Histoire économique et sociale de la France, vol. 2, 1660–1789* (Paris: Presses Universitaires de France, 1975), p. 85.

20. See the contemporary testimonies cited in Léon Abensour, *La Femme et le féminisme avant la Révolution* (Paris: Leroux, 1923; rpt. Geneva: Slatkine, 1977), p. 247; Edmonde Charles-Roux, *Les Femmes et le travail du moyen-âge à nos jours* (Paris: La Courtille, 1975), pp. 64–67.

21. See John Desmond Bernal, *Science in History*, 4 vols. (Harmondsworth: Penguin, 1969), vol. 2, p. 457.

22. de Puisieux, pp. 113–14. "[U]ne femme est aussi capable qu'un homme de s'instruire par le moyen d'une carte des bons & mauvais chemins des routes sures ou des dangereuses, & des positions propres pour un campement. Qui pourroit empêcher, qu'elle ne se mît au fait de tous les strategèmes de guerre, de la manière de charger l'ennemi, de faire une retraite, de méditer une surprise, de dresser des embuscades."

23. Ibid., pp. 110–11.

24. Ibid., p. 57.

25. 3 vols. (Amsterdam: Aux dépens de la Compagnie, 1753), BN R 24131–24134.

26. Ibid., vol. 2, pp. 56–263.

27. See Jules Delvailles, *Essai sur l'histoire de l'idée de progrès jusqu'à la fin du XVIIIᵉ siècle* (Geneva, 1910; rpt. Geneva: Slatkine, 1969); Werner Krauss, "Cartaud de la Villate und die Entstehung des geschichtlichen Weltbildes in der Frühaufklärung," in *Studien zur deutschen und französischen Aufklärung* (Berlin: Rütten & Loening, 1963), pp. 157–240; Johannes Rohbeck, *Die Fortschrittstheorie der Aufklärung: Französische und englische Geschichtsphilosophie in der zweiten Hälfte des 18. Jahrhunderts* (Frankfurt am Main: Campus, 1987).

28. Caffiaux, *Defenses* . . . , vol. 2, pp. 82–84.

29. Ibid., pp. 9–53.

30. *Dissertation sur la question lequel de l'homme ou de la femme est plus capable de constance, ou la Cause des dames, soutenue par Mlle Archambault de Laval, Bas-Maine, contre M.ˣˣˣ & M.L.L.R.* (Paris, 1750), BN R 24081.

31. Ibid., p. 9. "[L]a foiblesse & la fragilité ne doivent regarder que le corps de la femme, comme la force de l'homme au-dessus d'elle, ne doit s'étendre que de celle du corps."

32. Ibid., pp. 14–15. "[E]lles [les femmes] ont plus de mémoire, l'esprit plus docile, plus vif, plus pénétrant que la plupart des hommes, disent même leurs ennemis, le goût meilleur & plus sûre avec une grande justesse de discernement pour les choses fines et délicates."

33. Ibid., p. 37. "[M]ais suffisent-ils [les romans] pour s'arroger le titre de scavantes?"

34. Ibid., p. 35. "solidité de jugement, étendu d'esprit, justesse de raisonnement."

35. Ibid, pp. 39–40. "[U]ne femme qui fait dans sa sphère ce dont elle est capable, qui a soin de son domestique, qui s'applique à donner de bons commencemens d'éducation à ses enfants, qui règle sa maison, qui est soumise à son mari, mérite . . . autant de louanges que tous ces héros, tous ces grands politiques, & tous ces scavans."

36. See Paul Rousselot, *Histoire de l'education des femmes en France* (Paris: Didier, 1883), vol. 1, pp. 384–441; Renate Baader, *Dames de lettres: Autorinnen des preziösen, hocharistokratischen und "modernen" Salons, 1649–1698* (Stuttgart: Metzler, 1986), pp. 37–40.

37. Madame de Lambert, "Réflexions nouvelles sur les femmes," in *Œuvres*, ed. Robert Granderoute (Paris: Champion, 1990), pp. 213–37.

38. Lambert, *Réflexions*, p. 221.

39. Ibid., p. 220. "Je crois que le goût dépend de deux choses: d'un sentiment très délicat dans le cœur et d'une grande justesse dans l'esprit."

40. Ibid., p. 221. "[C]hez les femmes, les idées s'offrent d'elles-mêmes, et s'arrangent plutôt par sentiment que par réflexion: La nature *raisonne* [emphasis added] pour elles, et leur épargne tous les frais."

41. Ibid., p. 222. "[R]ien n'est si absolu que la supériorité de l'esprit qui vient de la sensibilité. . . ."

42. Ibid., p. 223. "La gloire, qui est l'âme et le soutien de toutes les productions de l'esprit, leur est refusée."

43. It is unclear exactly when the *Réflexions* were written. A number of indicators in the text point to the beginning of the Régence as the period of their composition. See Ginette Kryssing-Berg, "La Marquise de Lambert, ou l'ambivalence de la vertu," *Revue Romane* 17, no. 1 (1982), 35–48, 38. According to Emile Boulan, the two "Avis" were written around 1700. *Figures du dix-huitième siècle* (Leiden: Sijthoff, 1920), p. 113. Ellen McNiven Hine considers the year 1698 likely. "Mme de Lambert and her Circle: On the Threshold of a New Age," *Studies on Voltaire and the Eighteenth Century*, 102 (1973), pp. 173–91. See also Jeannette Geffriaud-Rosso, "Madame de Lambert," in *Etudes sur la féminité aux XVIIᵉ et XVIIIᵉ siècles* (Pisa: Goliardica, 1984), pp. 65–89. Robert Granderoute, the editor of the first critical edition of the works of Madame de Lambert, assumes that the *Réflexions* were completed before 1724. See Madame de Lambert, *Œuvres*, p. 208.

44. "Avis d'une mère à son fils," in *Œuvres* pp. 43–94; quotation on p. 45.

"Rien ne convient moins à un jeune homme qu'une certaine modestie qui lui fait croire qu'il n'est pas capable de grandes choses. Cette modestie est une langueur de l'âme qui l'empêche de prendre l'essor et de se porter avec rapidité vers la gloire."

45. "Avis d'une mère à sa fille," in *Œuvres* pp. 95–150; quotation on p. 104. "Que votre première parure soit donc la modestie." For an interpretation of the "Avis," see Ursula Böhmer, "Konversation und Literatur: Zur Rolle der Frau im französischen Salon im 18. Jahrhundert," in Baader and Fricke, *Die französische Autorin*, pp. 109–30, 121.

46. Lambert, "Avis d'une mère à sa fille," p. 111. "C'est la langue de l'amour."

47. Ibid., p. 112. "Songez que les filles doivent avoir sur les sciences une pudeur presque aussi tendre que sur les vices."

48. Renate Baader, "Die Literatur der Frau oder die Aufklärung der kleinen Schritte," in *Neues Handbuch der Literaturwissenschaft*, ed. Jürgen von Stackelberg (Wiesbaden: Athenaion, 1980), vol. 13, pp. 70–106; quoted on p. 87.

49. Ibid., p. 87.

Chapter 2

1. *Encyclopédie ou Dictionnaire raisonné des sciences, des arts et des métiers*, 35 vols. (Paris: Panckoucke, 1751–80; rpt. Stuttgart: Frommann, 1966–67). For a further discussion of women and the *Encyclopédie*, see my article "Qui peut définir les femmes? L'Idée de la 'nature féminine' au siècle des Lumières," in *Dix-huitième siècle* 26 (1994), 333–48.

2. *Encyclopédie*, vol. VIII, p. 274b. "HOMME (*Morale*), ce mot n'a de signification précise, qu'autant qu'il nous rappelle tout ce que nous sommes; mais ce que nous sommes ne peut pas être compris dans une définition; pour en montrer seulement une partie, il faut encore des divisions & des détails. Nous ne parlerons point ici de notre forme extérieure, ni de l'organisation qui nous range dans la classe des animaux. Voyez HOMME (*Anatomie*). *L'homme* que nous considérons est cet être qui pense, qui veut & qui agit."

3. Ibid., vol. VI, p. 468. "[F]emelle de l'homme."

4. Friederike Hassauer-Roos, "Das Weib und die Idee der Menschheit: Überlegungen zur neueren Geschichte der Diskurse über die Frau," in *Der Diskurs der Literatur- und Sprachhistorie*, ed. B. Cerquiglini and H. U. Gumbrecht (Frankfurt am Main: Suhrkamp, 1983), pp. 421–45, 428.

5. *Encyclopédie*, vol. VIII, p. 272.

6. Ibid., vol. VIII, pp. 274b–275a. "Mais toutes leurs [des bêtes] actions rassemblées laissent encore entr'elles & *l'homme* une distance infinie. Que l'empire qu'il a sur elles soit usurpé si l'on veut, il n'en est pas moins une preuve

de la supériorité de ses moyens, & par conséquent de sa nature. On ne peut qu'être frappé de cet avantage lorsqu'on regarde les travaux immenses de *l'homme*, qu'on examine le détail de ses arts, & le progrès de ses sciences; qu'on le voit franchir les mers, mesurer les cieux, & disputer au tonnerre son bruit & ses effets."

7. Article HOMME, *Encyclopédie*, vol. VIII, p. 256b. "[U]n être . . . qui paroït être à la tête de tous les autres animaux sur lesquels il domine."

8. On the history of the meaning of honnêteté, see H. Scheffers, *Höfische Konvention und die Aufklärung: Wandlungen des honnête-homme-Ideals im 17. und 18. Jahrhunderts* (Bonn: Bouvier, 1980), and M. Nerlich, *Kritik der Abenteuerideologie: Beitrag zur Erforschung der bürgerlichen Bewußtseinsbildung, 1100–1750* (Berlin: Akademie Verlag, 1977), vol. 1, pt. 2, pp. 485–526. See also Antoine Gombaud, Chevalier de Méré, *Discours de la vraie Honnêteté"* [1700], in *Œuvres complètes*, ed. Charles H. Boudhors (Paris: Roches, 1930), vol. 2.

9. *Encyclopédie*, vol. XI, p. 445.

10. Ibid.: "La pratique de l'oisivité est une chose contraire aux devoirs de l'homme et du citoyen, dont l'obligation générale est d'être bon à quelque chose, & en particulier de se rendre utile à la société dont il est membre. Rien ne peut dispenser personne de ce devoir, parce qu'il est imposé par la nature."

11. Léon Abensour, *La Femme et le féminisme avant la Révolution* (Paris: Leroux, 1923), pp. 151–249. Alongside women's complete integration into agricultural production, there was scarcely a sale contract in Paris or the Ile de France which was not signed by both the vendor and his wife. Even before Turgot's 1776 edict granting women access to all guilds, almost every city had a number of mixed guilds in addition to those with an exclusively female membership (laundresses, flower-sellers). Almost all wives either worked in their husband's workshops or sold their products in an adjacent shop. In most cases, widows were entitled to assume their late husband's master status and continue his business. In the cities, particularly Paris, whole legions of women were employed by rich households as cooks, chambermaids, or ladies' maids. Some luxury trades (dressmaking, jewelry) were largely in the hands of women who often led the lives of wealthy merchants.

12. *Encyclopédie*, vol. VII, p. 278b. "Il n'y a de véritables richesses que *l'homme* & la terre. *L'homme* ne vaut rien sans la terre, & la terre ne vaut rien sans *l'homme*. *L'homme* vaut par le nombre; plus une société est nombreuse, plus elle est puissante pendant la paix, plus elle est redoutable dans les tems de la guerre. Un souverain s'occupera donc sérieusement de la multiplication de ses sujets. Plus il aura de sujets, plus il aura de commerçans, d'ouvriers, de soldats."

13. Rolf Reichardt, "Bevölkerung und Gesellschaft Frankreichs im 18. Jahrhundert," *Zeitschrift für historische Forschung* 4 (1977), 154–221.

14. Jean-Louis Flandrin, *Families in Former Times: Kinship, Household,*

Sexuality, trans. Richard Southern (Cambridge: Cambridge UP, 1979), p. 185. The nonagricultural production sectors and the rapidly expanding service sector, which was gaining in economic significance, particularly in large cities like Paris, no longer functioned within the traditional production unit of the family—the "ganzes Haus," or "whole household." The spatial separation of paid work and family life brought with it a dissociation between tasks associated with reproduction (childcare, etc.) and productive labor. The old family structure, in which both husband and wife were integrated into the productive process, was not equal to this new division of labor. The burgeoning bourgeois economy destroyed the organic process of production and reproduction within the family unit, leaving women torn between the separating spheres of social production and individual reproduction. Cf. Hans Medick, "Zur strukturellen Fuktion von Haushalt und Familie im Übergang von der traditionellen Agrargesellschaft zum industriellen Kapitalismus: Die protoindustrielle Familienwirtschaft," in *Sozialgeschichte der Familie in der Neuzeit Europas*, ed. W. Conze (Stuttgart: Klett, 1976).

15. Elisabeth Badinter, *L'Amour en plus: Histoire de l'amour maternel* (Paris: Flammarion, 1983), pp. 141–53.

16. A few of the proverbs cited on the subject of women's worthlessness were: "Bonne *femme*, méchante bête; bonne mule, méchante tête"; "De *femme* & de fromage, qui en prend le moins, est le plus sage"; and "Si les femmes etoient d'argent, elles ne vaudroient rien a faire monnoie." *Supplément au Dictionnaire universel françois et latin* (Nancy: Chez Pierre Antoine, 1752), vol. I, col. 1088. The *Dictionnaire de Trévoux*, as it was popularly known, was first published in 1701 and went through several editions in the eighteenth century.

17. *Encyclopédie*, vol. VI, pp. 479b–481b.

18. Ibid., vol. X, p. 337.

19. Ibid., pp. 104a–106b; quoted on p. 105a. "Les années précieuses et trop bornées de la fécondité des femmes."

20. Article MARIAGE (*Droit nat.*), ibid., p. 106a. "La fin de la société entre le mâle & la femelle n'étant pas simplement de procréer mais de continuer l'espèce, cette société doit durer du moins même, après la procréeation, aussi long-tems qu'il est nécessaire pour la nourriture & la conservation des procréés, c'est-à-dire, jusqu'à ce qu'ils soient capables de pourvoir eux-mêmes à leurs besoins. En cela consiste la principale & peut-être la seule raison, pour laquelle le mâle & la femelle humains sont obligés à une société plus longue que n'entretiennent les autres animaux."

21. *Cahiers de doléances des femmes en 1789 et autres textes* (Paris: Edition des femmes, 1981).

22. *Encyclopédie*, vol. II, pp. 801b–807b.

23. Ibid., vol. XVII, p. 406b. "Ceux qui enseignent je ne sais quelle doctrine austere qui nous affligeroit sur la sensibilité d'organes que nous avons reçue de

la nature qui vouloit que la conservation de l'espèce & la nôtre fussent encore un objet de plaisirs; & sur cette foule d'objets qui nous entourent & qui sont destinés à emouvoir cette sensibilité en cent manières agréables, sont des atrabilaires à enfermer aux petites-maisons."

24. As Jaucourt remarks in the article SEXE (*Morale*) (*Encyclopédie*, vol. XV, p. 138a): "[L]e *sexe* absolument parlant, ou plutôt le beau-*sexe*, est l'épithète qu'on donne aux femmes."

25. See Badinter, *L'Amour en plus*, p. 190.

26. *Encyclopédie*, vol. I, p. 85b. "Il voudroit mieux pour les femmes . . . qu'il n'y eût point d'*Accoucheuses*. L'art des accouchements ne convient que lorsqu'il y a quelque obstacles: mais ces femmes n'attendent pas le tems de la nature; elles déchirent l'œuf, & elles arrachent l'enfant avant que la femme ait de vraies douleurs."

27. See Janet Sayers, *Biological Politics* (London and New York: Tavistock, 1982).

28. Article FEMME (*Morale*), *Encyclopédie*, vol. VI, p. 472a. "Si cette même délicatesse d'organes qui rend l'imagination des *femmes* plus vive, rend leur esprit moins capable d'attention, on peut dire qu'elles apperçoivent plus vîte, peuvent voir aussi bien, regardent moins longtems."

29. *Encyclopédie*, vol. X, p. 200a. "[L]e moindre dérangement de ce viscere est suivi d'un désordre universel dans toute la machine; on pourroit assurer qu'il n'est presque point de maladie chez les femmes où la matrice n'ait quelque part."

30. Ibid., p. 116b. "Dès lors emportées hors d'elles-mêmes, elles perdent de vûe toutes les lois de la pudeur, de la bienséance, cherchent par toutes sortes de moyens à assouvir la violence de leur passion; elles ne rougissent point d'attaquer les hommes, de les attirer par les postures les plus indécentes & les invitations les plus lascives."

31. Ibid. "Tous les practiciens conviennent que les différens symptomes de vapeurs ou d'affections hystériques qui attaquent les filles ou les veuves, sont une suite de la privation du mariage."

32. Ibid. "Les Médecins sont souvent obligés de faire marier ces malades, & le succès du remède constate la bonté du conseil. . . . Il est mille occasions où le coït légitimé par le mariage n'est pas possible; & la religion ne permet pas alors d'imiter l'heureuse témérité de Rolfink, qui ne voyant d'autre ressource pour guérir une fille dangereusement malade, que de procurer l'excrétion de la semence: au défaut d'un mari, il se servit dans ce dessein, d'un moyen artificiel, & la guérit entièrement."

33. *Encyclopédie*, vol. VI, p. 473b. "Elles [les femmes] semblent n'avoir été formées que pour le doux emploi d'aimer."

34. Ibid., p. 474b. "Plus que galante, elle croit cependant n'être que coquette. C'est dans cette persuasion qu'à une table de jeu, alternativement attentive & distraite, elle répond du genou à l'un, serre la main à l'autre en louant ses

dentelles, & jette en même tems quelques mots convenus à un troisième. Elle se
dit sans préjugés, parce qu'elle est sans principes; elle s'arroge le titre d'*honnête
homme*, parce qu'elle a renoncé à celui d'*honnête femme*."

35. Ibid., p. 474a. "[E]lle sait donner à la volupté toutes les apparences du
sentiment, à la complaisance tous les charmes de la volupté. Elle sait également
& dissimuler des désirs & feindre des sentimens, & composer des ris & verser
des larmes. Elle a rarement dans l'ame ce qu'elle a dans les yeux; elle n'a presque
jamais sur les lèvres, ni ce qu'elle a dans les yeux, ni ce qu'elle a dans l'ame."

36. Ibid., p. 472a. "Qui peut définir les femmes? Tout à la verité parle en
elles, mais un langage équivoque. . . . Il en est de l'ame des femmes comme de
leur beauté; il semble qu'elle ne fassent appercevoir que pour laisser imaginer!"

37. Ibid., p. 475a. "[S]on bonheur est d'ignorer ce que le monde appelle *les
plaisirs*, sa gloire est de vivre ignorée. Renfermée dans les devoirs de femme &
de mère, elle consacre ses jours à la pratique des vertus obscures: occupée du
gouvernement de sa famille, elle regne sur son mari par la complaisance, sur ces
enfans par la douceur, sur ses domestiques par la bonté: sa maison est la demeure
des sentimens religieux, de la piété filiale, de l'amour conjugal, de la tendresse
maternelle, de l'ordre, de la paix intérieure, du doux sommeil, & de la santé:
économe & sédentaire, elle en écarte les passions & les besoins; l'indigent qui
se présente à sa porte, n'en est jamais repoussé; l'homme licentieux ne s'y
présente point. Elle a un caractère de réserve & de dignité qui la fait respecter,
d'indulgence & de sensibilité qui la fait aimer, de prudence et de fermeté qui la
fait craindre; elle répand autour d'elle une douce chaleur, une lumière pure qui
éclaire & vivifie tout ce qui l'environne. Est-ce la nature qui l'a placée ou la
raison qui l'a conduite au rang suprême où je la vois?"

38. Cf. the articles COLLEGE (vol. III, pp. 633a–638), ÉDUCATION (vol. V, pp.
397a–403a), and ÉTUDE (vol. VI, pp. 86a–97b).

39. Cf. the article SEXE (*Morale*) by Jaucourt, vol. XV, p. 138a. "[M]ais la
culture de leur esprit est encore plus importante et essentielle."

40. Article FEMME (*Anthropologie*), vol. VI, p. 469b. "[C]ette étude cause
des distractions qui affoiblissent les penchans vicieux."

41. Ibid, p. 475a. "Il est une femme qui a de l'esprit pour se faire aimer, non
pour se faire craindre."

42. Ibid., p. 472a. "On doit être surpris que des ames si incultes puissent
produire tant de vertus, & qu'il n'y germe plus de vice."

43. Silvia Bovenschen, *Die imaginierte Weiblichkeit: Exemplarische Untersuchungen zu kulturgeschichtlichen und literarischen Präsentationsformen des
Weiblichen* (Frankfort am Main: Suhrkamp, 1979), pp. 84–91.

44. Article FEMME (*Anthropologie*), vol. VI, p. 469b. "[Q]ue l'étude des lettres
éclaire, & donne une sagesse qu'on n'achète point par les secours dangereux de
l'expérience. . . . Mais on pourroit douter si cette prudence précoce ne coûte point
un peu d'innocence."

45. See, among others, the articles HONNÊTE (vol. VIII, pp. 286–287b); SOCIABILITÉ (vol. XV, pp. 250b–251b); MANIÈRE (vol. X, pp. 34b–36b); and SOCIÉTÉ, vol. XV, pp. 252a–259a, esp. p. 253b. Jacques Proust sees the "goût pour les arts utiles" of the "bourgeoisie encyclopédique" as a characteristic setting them apart from fashionable society, a criterion I find useful in differentiating between the sociability of the socially very heterogeneous Encyclopedists and the "gens du monde." See Jacques Proust, *L'Encyclopédie* (Paris: Colin, 1965), pp. 98–99.

Chapter 3

1. Antoine Léonard Thomas, *Essai sur le caractère, les mœurs et l'esprit des femmes dans les differents siècles* (Paris: Moutard, 1772). I cite here from this edition. The *Essai* is now available in a modern edition, in *Qu'est-ce qu'une femme?* Elisabeth Badinter, ed. (Paris: P.O.L., 1989). Pierre Roussel, *Système physique et moral de la femme, ou tableau philosophique de la constitution, de l'état organique, du tempérament, des mœurs, & des fonctions propres au sexe* (Paris: Vincent, 1775), BN Tb^{12}3. Reviews of Thomas appeared in the *Journal encyclopédique* 5 (1772), 364–76 and 1 (1773), 108–16; the *Mercure* II (July 1773); *Année littéraire* 4 (1774), 145–183. It is still reviewed in the *Grand Dictionnaire Universel Larousse* of 1865–76, vol. VIII, p. 28.

2. Thomas, *Essai*, p. 38. "Il faudroit voir . . . jusqu'à quel degré . . . la foiblesse naturelle de leurs [les femmes] organes . . . leur permet cette attention forte & soutenue qui peut combiner de suite une longue chaine d'idées."

3. Roussel, *Système*, pp. x–xi. "[A]près avoir consideré la femme par son côté physique, je l'ai examiné par son côté moral. En cela j'ai, sans doute, rappelé la médecine à ses véritables droits. J'ai toujours été persuadé que ce n'est que dans son sein qu'on peut trouver les fondements de la bonne morale. . . ."

4. See Klaus Dörner, *Bürger und Irre: Zur Sozialgeschichte und Wissenschaftssoziologie der Psychiatrie* (Frankfurt am Main: Fischer, 1975), pp. 121–24. English trans. Joachim Neugroschel and Jean Steinberg, *Madmen and the Bourgeoisie: A Social History of Insanity and Psychiatry* (Oxford: Basil Blackwell, 1984).

5. René Descartes, *Traité de l'homme*, in *Œuvres et lettres*, ed. André Bridoux (Paris: Gallimard, 1958), pp. 807–73.

6. "This great source of most of the ideas we have, depending wholly upon our senses, and derived by them to understanding, I call SENSATION." John Locke, *An Essay Concerning Human Understanding*, ed. John W. Yolton, 2 vols. (London: J. M. Dent, 1961), vol. 1, p. 78. Etienne Bonnot de Condillac, *Essai sur l'origine des connaissances humaines*, in *Œuvres complètes* (Paris 1821–22; rpt. Geneva: Slatkine, 1970), vol. 1, pp. 1–392.

7. Locke, *Essay*, vol. 1, p. 78.

8. Roussel, *Système*, p. 22. "[E]ffets immédiats qui paroissent dériver de l'organisation des Parties sensibles de la femme."

9. Ibid., p. 30. "[L]a difficulté de se dérober à la tyrannie des sensations l'attachant continuellement aux causes immédiates qui les produisent, ne lui permettent point de s'élever à la hauteur convenable pour les embrasser toutes d'une seule vue."

10. Thomas, *Essai*, pp. 80–81. "On a mis par-tout l'autorité à la place du raisonnement, même quand on a parlé des femmes, mais en pareille matière, comme en beaucoup d'autres, vingt citations ne valent pas une raison!"

11. Ibid., p. 81. "Il semble que pour terminer cette grande question d'amour propre de rivalité entre les deux sexes, il faudroit examiner la force ou la faiblesse des organes."

12. Ibid., p. 82.

13. Ibid., pp. 83–84. "Il [l'esprit des femmes] a plus de saillies que d'efforts. Ce qu'il n'a pas vu en un instant, ou il ne le voit pas ou il le dédaigne, ou il désespère de le voir. Il seroit donc moins étonnant qu'elles n'eussent point cette opiniâtre lenteur, qui seule recherche & découvre les grandes vérités."

14 . Ibid., p. 82. "[F]oiblesse naturelle de leurs organes, d'où résulte leur beauté . . . l'inquiétude de leur caractère, qui tient à leur imagination . . . la multitude & la variété des sensations, qui fait une partie de leurs graces."

15. Ibid., p. 87. "[E]sprit d'ordre & de mémoire qui classe les faits & des idées afin de les retrouver au besoin."

16. Ibid., p. 88. "On sait qu'il y a des qualités d'esprit qui s'excluent. Ce ne peut être la même main qui taille le diamant, & qui creuse la mine."

17. Joseph Raulin, *Traité des affections vaporeuses du sexe avec l'exposition de leurs symptômes, de leurs différentes causes et la méthode de les guérir* (Paris: J. T. Hérissant, 1758), BN Td 85.56.

18. Roussel, *Système*, p. 103. "Leurs organes délicats se ressentiroient davantage les inconvéniens inévitables qu'elle [une étude sérieuse] entraîne!"

19. Ibid., pp. 103–4. "Les hommes qui veulent flatter les femmes, disent . . . que nous leur fermons la porte des sciences, pour nous assurer exclusivement ce genre de supériorité. Ce qu'il y a de plus vrai c'est qu'elles ne s'en soucient guere; & c'est avec raison. On veut les louer sur l'esprit qu'elles pourroient avoir, comme s'il n'y avoit point d'éloges à donner à celui qu'elles ont."

20. Ibid., p. 102. "Une personne profondément occupée n'existe que par la tête; elle semble à peine respirer. Le corps privé des sucs qui le renouvellent . . . languit, se fane & tombe comme un tendre arbrisseau planté dans un terrain aride, & dont l'ardeur du soleil a desséché les branches."

21. Thomas, *Essai*, p. 84. "Leurs sens mobiles [qui] parcourent tous les objets & en emportent l'image. . . . Le monde réel ne leur suffit pas; elles aiment à se créer un monde imaginaire; elles l'habitent & l'embelissent."

22. Ibid. "Les spectres, les enchantemens, les prodiges, tout ce qui sort des

loix ordinaires de la nature, sont leurs ouvrages & leurs délices. Leur ame s'exalte & leur esprit est toujours plus près de l'enthousiasme."

Chapter 4

1. Michel Delon, "Le Prétexte anatomique," *Dix-huitième siècle* 12 (1980), 35–48; and J.-M. Goulemot, "Prêtons la main à la nature," Ibid, pp. 97–111.

2. Delon, "Le Prétexte anatomique," 36. "La femme est définie par rapport à l'homme comme manque, comme excédent ou, selon une théorie plus elaborée, comme inversion."

3. The ovaries, for example, were referred to as "testicules." See Elisabeth Fontenay, "Diderot gynéconome," *Digraphe* 7 (1976), 38.

4. Cited in Fontenay, "Diderot gynéconome," 38. "[E]n réfléchissant sur la structure des parties de la génération de l'un et l'autre sexe dans l'espèce humaine, on y trouve tant de ressemblance et une conformité si singulière qu'on serait assez porté à croire que les parties qui nous paraissent si différentes à l'extérieur ne sont au fond que les mêmes organes."

5. *Encyclopédie*, vol. VI, pp. 468b–469a. "M. Daubenton . . . après avoir remarqué la plus grande analogie entre les deux sexes pour la secrétion & l'emission de la semence, croit que toute la différence que l'ont peut trouver dans la grandeur & la position de certaines parties, dépend de la matrice qu'est plus dans les femmes que dans les hommes, & que ce viscere rendroit les organes de la génération dans les hommes absolument semblables à ceux des femmes, s'il en faisoit partie."

6. Pierre Roussel, *Système physique et moral de la femme* (Paris: Vincent, 1775), pp. iv–v. "Si d'un côté les philosophes ont bien observé le moral, d'un autre, les médecins ont bien développé le physique, du moins autant qu'il est possible. Il eût été seulement à désirer que ces derniers se fussent un peu plus arrêtés sur la constitution générale de la femme, & n'eussent point paru la regarder comme un être semblable en tout à l'homme, excepté dans les fonctions particulières qui caracterisent le sexe."

7. Ibid, pp. 133–34. "Il y a des auteurs qui ont cru voir beaucoup de ressemblances entre les parties génitales de femme et celles de l'homme. . . . On peut être assuré que ces auteurs ont été séduits par des rapports faux ou peu approfondis. La seule différence des fonctions de l'homme & de la femme, dans l'œuvre importante de la génération, suffit pour éloigner toute idée de similitude entre les organes par lesquels chacun d'eux y coopère."

8. Ibid., p. 17. "Il est donc vraisemblable que la disposition des parties qui composent le corps de la femme, est déterminée par la nature même, & qu'elle sert de *fondement* [emphasis added] au caractere physique & moral qui la distingue."

9. Denis Diderot, *Sur les femmes*, in *Œuvres*, ed. André Billy (Paris: Gallimard, 1951), pp. 949–58.

10. Ibid., p. 950. "Moins maîtresses de leurs sens que nous, la récompense en est moins prompte et moins sûre pour elles."

11.. Ibid., p. 953. "La femme dominée par l'hystérisme éprouve je ne sais quoi d'infernal ou de céleste. Quelquefois, elle m'a fait frissoner. C'est dans la fureur de la bête féroce qui fait partie d'elle-même, que je l'ai vue, que je l'ai entendue."

12. Ibid., p. 952. "La femme porte au-dedans d'elle-même un organe susceptible de spasmes terribles, disposant d'elle, et suscitant dans son imagination des fantômes de toute espèce. . . . C'est de l'organe propre à son sexe que partent toutes ses idées extraordinaires."

13. Ibid., p. 957. "[P]lus civilisées que nous en dehors, elles sont restées de vraies sauvages en dedans, toutes machiavélistes, du plus au moins."

14 . Ibid., pp. 956–57. "[F]aute de réflexion et de principes, rien ne pénètre jusqu'à une certaine profondeur de conviction dans l'entendement des femmes; que les idées de justice, de vertu, de vice, de bonté, de méchanceté nagent à la superficie de leur âme."

15. Ibid., p. 957. "Le symbole des femmes en général est celle de l'Apocalypse sur le front de laquelle il est écrit: MYSTÈRE."

16. Fontenay, "Diderot gynéconome," 34. "C'est en amant qu'écrit Diderot, non en sujet d'un savoir, non en stratège de la séduction ou en vicaire du divin censeur. . . . Ainsi doit s'interpréter la référence insistante à la première personne du masculin pluriel: loin de se donner pour une norme à laquelle les femmes feraient exception elle souligne l'engagement du désir de l'homme dans son discours sur la femme."

17. Ibid., p. 47. "La matrice permet à Diderot de mettre au point le stratagème anti-cartésien, en ce que les divagations de sa fureur, comme les ruses de ses simulacres, menacent l'apanage d'une autre expérience, celle, ponctuelle de recueillement de la substance pensante, et de l'unicité du sujet. L'Hystérisme pantomime affole l'idée claire et distincte, brouille l'évidence et raille la vérité: la singularité féminine déboute l'universel masculin."

18. Michèle Duchet, "Du sexe des livres: 'Sur les femmes' de Diderot," *Revue des sciences humaines* 168 (1977), 525–36; quotation on p. 527. "[L]a véritable hardiesse de Diderot n'est pas cette théorie du corps féminin. . . . Elle est tout entière dans le lien qu'il établit entre le physique, le moral et la production des idées chez des êtres ainsi abandonées à la discrétion d'un organe, qui détermine leur comportement et dérègle leurs conduites."

19. Joseph Raulin, *Traité des affections vaporeuses du sexe* (Paris: J. T. Hérissant, 1758).

20. Diderot, *Sur les femmes*, 956. "Quand on écrit des femmes, il faut tremper sa plume dans l'arc-en-ciel et jeter sur la ligne la poussière des ailes du papil-

lon; comme le petit chien du pèlerin, à chaque fois qu'on secoue la patte il faut qu'en tombe des perles; et il n'en tombe point de celle de M. Thomas."

21. Robert Mauzi, Introduction to Denis Diderot, *La Religieuse* (Paris: Colin, 1961), pp. vii–xxxvii; quotation on p. xii.

22. Denis Diderot, *La Religieuse*, in *Œuvres*, pp. 235–394.

23. Denis Diderot, *The Nun*, trans. Leonard Tancock (Harmondsworth: Penguin, 1974), p. 142. *La Religieuse*, pp. 348–49. "'Noyer de larmes ces yeux! . . .' et elle les baisait. 'Arracher la plainte et le gémissement de cette bouche! . . .' Et elle la baisait. 'Condamner ce visage charmant et serein à se couvrir sans cesse des nuages de tristesse! . . .' Et elle le baisait. . . . 'Oser entourer ce cou d'une corde, et déchirer ces épaules avec des pointes aiguës! . . .' Et elle écartait mon linge de cou et de tête; elle entr'ouvrait le haut de ma robe. . . ."

24. *The Nun*, p. 140. "[E]lle est capable de passer de la plus grande sensibilité jusqu'à la férocité." *La Religieuse*, p. 346.

25. *The Nun*, p. 174. "Que la condition d'un religieux, d'une religieuse qui n'est point appelée, est fâcheuse! c'est la nôtre, pourtant; et nous ne pouvons la changer. On nous a chargés de chaînes pesantes, que nous sommes condamnés à secouer sans cesse, sans aucun espoir de les rompre; tâchons, chère soeur, de les traîner." *La Religieuse*, p. 379.

26. Diderot, "Sur les femmes," p. 953. "[L]a recluse dans la cellule se sent élever dans les airs; son âme répand dans le sein de la Divinité; son essence se mêle à l'essence divine; elle se pâme; elle se meurt; sa poitrine s'élève et s'abaisse avec rapidité; ses compagnes, attroupées autour d'elle, coupent les lacets de son vêtement qui la serre. La nuit vient; elle entend les choeurs célestes; sa voix s'unit à leurs concerts. Ensuite elle redescend sur la terre; elle parle de joies ineffables; on l'écoute; elle est convaincue; elle persuade."

27. *The Nun*, p. 172. "[E]lle jeûnait trois jours de la semaine; elle se macérait, elle entendait l'office dans les stalles inférieures. Il fallait passer devant sa porte pour aller à l'église; là nous la trouvions prosternée, le visage contre terre, et elle ne se relevait que quand il n'y avait plus personne. La nuit, elle descendait en chemise nu-pieds; si Sainte-Thérèse ou moi nous la rencontrions par hasard, elle se retournait et se collait le visage contre le mur. Un jour que je sortais de ma cellule, je la trouvais prosternée, les bras étendus et la face contre terre; et elle me dit: 'Avancez, marchez, foulez-moi aux pieds; je ne mérite pas un autre traitement.'" *La Religieuse*, pp. 377–78.

28. *The Nun*, p. 102. "Dieu, qui à créé l'homme sociable, approuve-t-il qu'il se renferme? Dieu qui l'a créé si inconstant, si fragile, peut-il autoriser la témérité de ses voeux? . . . Toutes ces cérémonies lugubres qu'on observe à la prise d'habit et à la profession, quand on consacre un homme ou une femme à la vie monastique et au malheur, suspendent-elles les fonctions animales?" *La Religieuse*, p. 311.

29. *The Nun*, p. 102. "Quel besoin a l'époux de tant de vierges folles?" *La Religieuse*, p. 310.

30. Denis Diderot, *Supplément au voyage de Bougainville*, in *Œuvres*, pp. 963–1002.

31. Otis Fellows has pointed to parallels between the two narratives both in narrative structure and in the portrayal of father figures and sexuality. See his essay "Diderot's 'Supplément' as a Pendant for 'La Religieuse,'" in *Literature and History in the Age of Ideas: Essays on the French Enlightenment, Presented to George Remington Havens*, ed. Charles G. Williams (Columbus: Ohio State UP, 1975), pp. 229–43.

32. K.-H. Kohl, *Der entzauberte Blick: Das Bild vom guten Wilden und die Erfahrung der Zivilisation* (Berlin: Medusa, 1981), pp. 231f.

33. See also Hans Hinterhäuser, *Utopie und Wirklichkeit bei Diderot: Studien zum 'Supplément au voyage de Bougainville'* (Heidelberg: Winter, 1957).

34. See Paul Hoffmann, *La Femme dans la pensée des Lumières* (Paris: Ophrys, 1977), p. 355.

35. See Herbert Dieckmann's Introduction to his edition of Diderot's *Supplément au voyage de Bougainville* (Geneva: Droz, 1951), p. cix.

Chapter 5

1. Werner Krauss, *Zur Anthropologie des 18. Jahrhunderts: Die Frühgeschichte der Menschheit im Blickpunkt der Aufklärung* (Munich: Hanser, 1979), p. 11.

2. See Michèle Duchet, *Anthropologie et histoire au siècle des lumières* (Paris: Maspero, 1971), and Urs Bitterli, *Die "Wilden" und die "Zivilisierten"* (Munich: C. H. Beck, 1982).

3. Duchet, *Anthropologie*. Werner Krauss, too, limits himself to a few thematic studies of the history of the word field "woman." *Zur Anthropologie*, pp. 120–22.

4. Elisabeth de Fontenay expressly argues that we should consider Rousseau's statements on women separately from his philosophy, in order to demonstrate more clearly the misogynist nature of his ideas on women: "Nous autres femmes, aussi cher que cela puisse nous coûter, nous devons, pour faire face à l'urgence, accepter parfois de sacrifier les philosophes et les poètes. . . ." "Pour Emile et par Emile, Sophie ou l'invention du ménage," *Les Temps Modernes* 358 (May 1976), 1774–95; quotation on p. 1776. Michelle Coquillat adopts a similar approach in *La Poètique du mâle* (Paris: Gallimard, 1982). On Rousseau, see pp. 164–81 in particular. For a social-historical interpretation of Rousseau, see Eva-Maria Knapp-Tepperberg, "Rousseaus 'Emile ou de l'Education'—Sexualauffassung und Bild der Frau: Ein Kapitel zur Antinomie des bürgerlichen Freiheitsbegriffs," *Romanistische Zeitschrift für Literaturgeschichte* (1978), 199–223. The author regards the differences between the upbringing of boys

and girls as one of degree only. In her view, the decisive characteristic of this upbringing is a restrictive sexual education which leads to "mutilations in the economy of drives." She cites "economic conditions" as the underlying reason (213).

5. *Discours qui a remporté le prix à l'Académie de Dijon sur cette question proposée: Si le rétablissement des Sciences & des Arts a contribué à épurer les mœurs*, 1750; and *Discours sur l'origine et les fondements de l'inégalité parmi les hommes*, 1755. All French quotations in the notes are based on the bilingual French-German edition, Jean-Jacques Rousseau, *Schriften zur Kulturkritik*, ed. Kurt Weigand, (Hamburg: Meiner, 1955).

6. Silvia Bovenschen, *Die imaginierte Weiblichkeit* (Frankfurt am Main: Suhrkamp, 1979), p. 173.

7. Ibid.

8. Jean-Jacques Rousseau, *Emile ou de l'éducation*, in *Œuvres complètes*, ed. Bernard Gagnebin and Marcel Raymond. (Paris: Gallimard, 1969), vol. 4, pp. 241–868; quotation on pp. 709–10. English trans. *Emile*, trans. Barbara Foxley (London: J. M. Dent, 1957), p. 332.

9. *Emile*, English trans., p. 349. "La recherche des vérités abstraites et spéculatives, des principes, des axiomes dans les sciences, tout ce qui tend à généraliser les idées n'est point au ressort des femmes: leurs études doivent se rapporter toutes à la pratique; c'est à elles à faire application des principes que l'homme à trouvés, et c'est à elles de faire les observations qui mènent l'homme à l'établissement des principes. Toutes les réflexions des femmes, en ce qui ne tient pas immédiatement à leurs devoirs, doivent tendre à l'étude des hommes ou aux connoissances agréables qui n'ont que le goût pour objet; car quant aux ouvrages de génie ils passent leur portée." *Emile*, pp. 736–37.

10. English trans., p. 338. "Par l'industrie et les talens le goût se forme; par le goût l'esprit s'ouvre insensiblement aux idées du beau dans tous les genres, et enfin aux notions morales qui s'y rapportent. C'est peut-être une des raisons pourquoi le sentiment de la décence et de l'honnêteté s'insinue plus tôt chez les filles que chez les garçons." *Emile*, p. 718.

11. English trans., p. 338. "Est-ce, par exemple, que l'art de chanter tient à la musique écrite? Ne sauroit-on rendre sa voix flexible et juste, apprendre à chanter avec goût, même à s'accompagner, sans connoître une seule note?" *Emile*, p. 717.

12. English trans., p. 339. "L'homme dit ce qu'il sait, la femme dit ce qui plait; l'un pour parler a besoin de connoissance et l'autre de goût." *Emile*, p. 718.

13. English trans., p. 346. "[L]'homme, *instruit* des gens qui se conviennent, les placera selon ce qu'il sait; la femme *sans rien savoir* ne s'y trompera pas. Elle aura déja lû dans les yeux, dans le maintien toutes les convenances, et chacun se trouvera placé comme il veut l'être." *Emile*, p. 732; emphasis added.

14. English trans., p. 348. "Or, cet art s'apprend-il? Non, il naît avec les

femmes; elles l'ont toutes, et jamais les hommes ne l'ont au même dégré. Tel est un des caractères distinctifs du sexe." *Emile*, p. 734.

15. English trans., p. 350. "Ils [les hommes] philosopheront mieux qu'elle [la femme] sur le cœur humain; mais elle lira mieux qu'eux dans les cœurs des hommes. C'est aux femmes à trouver, pour ainsi dire, la morale expérimentale, à nous à la réduire en sistême." *Emile*, p. 737.

16. English trans., p. 339. "[Q]uoi qu'il en soit du caractère des femmes, leur politesse est moins fausse que la nôtre, elle ne fait qu'étendre leur prémier instinct. . . ." *Emile*, p. 719.

17. English trans., p. 333. *Emile*, p. 711.

18. English trans., p. 339. "[L]'un doit avoir pour objet principal les choses utiles, l'autre [la femme] les agréables. Leurs discours ne doivent avoir des formes communes que celle de la vérité." *Emile*, p. 718.

19. English trans., p. 305. "Le goût ne s'éxerce que sur les choses indifférentes ou d'un intérest d'amusement tout au plus, et non sur celles qui tiennent à nos besoins; pour juger de celles-ci le goût n'est pas nécessaire, le seul appétit suffit." *Emile*, p. 671.

20. English trans., p. 306. *Emile*, p. 672.

21. English trans., p. 339. "Je remarque en général dans le commerce du monde, que la politesse des hommes est plus officieuse, et celle des femmes plus caressante. Cette différence n'est point d'institution, elle est naturelle. L'homme paroit chercher davantage à vous servir et la femme à vous agréer. Il suit de là que, quoi qu'il en soit du caractére des femmes, leur politesse est moins fausse que la nôtre, elle ne fait qu'étendre leur prémier instinct; mais quand un homme feint de préférer mon intérest au sien propre, de quelque démonstration qu'il colore son mensonge, je suis sur qu'il en fait un." *Emile*, p. 719.

22. On this, see Werner Krauss, *Cartaud de la Villate: Ein Beitrag zur Entstehung des geschichtlichen Weltbildes in der französischen Aufklärung*, 2 vols. (Berlin: Rütten & Loening, 1960), esp. vol. 1, pp. 78–79, and Hans Robert Jauss, "Ästhetische Normen und geschichtliche Reflexion in der Querelle des Anciens et des Modernes," Introduction to *Charles Perrault: Parallèle des anciens et des modernes en ce qui regarde les arts et les sciences*, ed. H. R. Jauss (Munich: Eidos, 1964), pp. 43ff.

23. On eighteenth-century English moral philosophy, see Philip Mercer, *Sympathy and Ethics: A Study of the Relationship Between Sympathy and Morality, with Special Reference to Hume's 'Treatise'* (Oxford: Clarendon, 1972). On the concept of moral sensibility as instinct, see Jean-Jacques Rousseau, *Lettre morale No. 5*, in *Œuvres complètes*, vol. 4, pp. 1106–11.

24. Jean-Jacques Rousseau, *A Discourse on the Origin of Inequality*, in *The Social Contract and Discourses*, trans. G. D. H. Cole, rev. J. H. Brumlett and John C. Hall (London: J. M. Dent, 1973), pp. 27–113; quotation on p. 87. "[E]n

un mot, concurrence et rivalité d'une part, de l'autre opposition d'intérêts, et toujours le désir caché de faire son profit aux dépens d'autrui. Tous ces maux sont le premier effet de la propriété et le cortège inséparable de l'inégalité naissante." Rousseau, *Discours*, p. 220.

25. *Discourse on Inequality*, p. 81. "A mesure que les idées et les sentiments se succèdent, que l'esprit et le cœur s'exercent, le genre humain continue à s'apprivoiser; les liaisons s'étendent, et les liens se resserrent. On s'accoutume à s'assembler devant les cabanes ou autour d'un grand arbre; le chant et la danse, vrais enfants de l'amour et du loisir, devinrent l'amusement ou plutôt l'occupation des hommes et des femmes oisifs et attroupés." *Discours*, p. 204.

26. *Discourse on Inequality*, p. 77. "Le long de la mer et des rivières, ils inventèrent la ligne et l'hameçon, et devinrent pêcheurs et ichthyophages. Dans les fôrets, ils se firent des arcs et des flèches, et devinrent chasseurs et guerriers. Dans les pays froids, ils se couvrirent des peaux des bêtes qu'ils avaient tuées. Le tonnerre, un volcan, ou quelque heureux hasard, leur fit connaître le feu, nouvelle ressource contre la rigueur de l'hiver: ils apprirent à conserver cet élément, puis à le reproduire, et enfin à en préparer les viandes qu'auparavant ils dévoraient crues. Cette application réitérée des êtres divers à lui-même, et des uns aux autres, dut naturellement engendrer dans l'esprit de l'homme les perceptions de certains rapports. Ces relations que nous exprimons par les mots de grand, de petit, de fort, de faible, de vite, de lent, de peureux, de hardi, et d'autres idées pareilles, comparées au besoin, et presque sans y songer, produisirent enfin chez lui quelque sorte de réflexion." *Discours*, p. 194.

27. Johannes Rohbeck, *Die Fortschrittsideologie der Aufklärung: Französische und englische Geschichtsphilosophie in der zweiten Hälfte des 18. Jahrhunderts* (Frankfurt am Main: Campus, 1987).

28. Iring Fetscher, *Rousseaus politische Philosophie* (Frankfurt am Main: Suhrkamp, 1981), p. 81.

29. *Discourse on Inequality*, p. 68. "C'est la raison qui engendre l'amour-propre, et c'est la réflexion qui la fortifie; c'est elle qui replie l'homme sur lui-même: c'est elle qui le sépare de tout ce qui le gêne et l'afflige. C'est la philosophie qui l'isole; c'est par elle qu'il dit en secret, à l'aspect d'un homme souffrant: 'Péris, si tu veux; je suis en sûreté.'" *Discours*, p. 174.

30. See also Victor Goldschmidt, *Anthropologie et politique: Les Principes du système de Rousseau* (Paris: Vrin, 1974), p. 297.

31. *Discourse on Inequality*, p. 55. "Quoi qu'en disent les moralistes, l'entendement humain doit beaucoup aux passions, qui, d'un commun aveu, lui doivent beaucoup aussi. C'est par leur activité que notre raison se perfectionne; nous ne cherchons à connaître que parce que nous désirons de jouir; et il n'est pas possible de concevoir pourquoi celui qui n'aurait ni désirs ni craintes se donnerait la peine de raisonner. Les passions à leur tour tirent leur origine de nos besoins, et leur progrès de nos connaissances. Car on ne peut désirer ou

craindre les choses que sur les idées qu'on en peut avoir, ou par la simple impulsion de la nature; et l'homme sauvage, privé de toute sorte de lumière, n'éprouve que les passions de cette dernière espèce; ses désirs ne passent pas ses besoins physiques." *Discours*, p. 134.

32. *Discourse on Inequality*, p. 80. "[E]t ce fut alors que s'établit la première différence dans la manière de vivre des deux sexes qui jusqu'ici n'en avait eu qu'une. Les femmes devinrent plus sédentaires et s'accoutumèrent à garder la cabane et les enfants, tandis que l'homme allait chercher la subsistence commune." *Discours*, p. 200.

33. Discourse on Inequality, pp. 79–80. "Les premiers développements du cœur furent l'effet d'une situation nouvelle qui réunissait dans une habitation commune les maris et les femmes, les pères et les enfants. L'habitude de vivre ensemble fit naître les plus doux sentiments qui soient connus des hommes, l'amour conjugal et l'amour paternel. Chaque famille devint une petite société d'autant mieux unie, que l'attachement réciproque et la liberté en étaient les seuls liens." *Discours*, p. 200.

34. *Emile*, English trans., pp. 371–72. "Au dehors elle est toujours ridicule et très justement critiquée, parce qu'on ne peut manquer de l'être aussitôt qu'on sort de son état et qu'on n'est point fait pour celui qu'on veut prendre. Toutes ces femmes à grands talens n'en imposent jamais qu'aux sots. On sait toujours quel est l'artiste ou l'ami qui tient la plume ou le pinceau quand elles travaillent. On sait quel est le discret homme de lettres qui leur dicte en secret leurs oracles. Toute cette charlatanerie est indigne d'une honnête femme." *Emile*, p. 768.

35. Fetscher, *Rousseaus politische Philosophie*, p. 82.

36. Ibid., p. 89.

37. *Emile*, English trans., p. 332. "[I]l faut les [les filles] exercer d'abord à la contrainte, afin qu'elle ne leur coûte jamais rien à dompter toutes leurs fantaisies pour les soumettre aux volontés d'autruis. Si elles vouloient toujours travailler on devroit quelquefois les forcer à ne rien faire. La dissipation, la frivolité, l'inconstance, sont des défauts qui naissent aisément de leurs premiers goûts corrompus et toujours suivis. Pour prévenir cet abus apprenez-leur surtout à se vaincre." *Emile*, p. 709.

38. *Emile*, English trans., p. 371. "D'ailleurs, comment une femme qui n'a nulle habitude de réfléchir élevera-t-elle ses enfans? Comment discernera-t-elle ce qui leur convient? Comment les disposera-t-elle aux vertus qu'elle ne connoît pas, au mérite dont elle n'a nulle idée?" *Emile*, p. 767.

39. *Emile*, English trans., pp. 345–46. "Je ne blâmerois pas sans distinction qu'une femme fut bornée aux seuls travaux de son sexe et qu'on la laissât dans une profonde ignorance sur tout le reste; mais il faudroit pour cela des mœurs publiques très simples, très saines, ou une manière de vivre très retirée. Dans de grandes villes et parmi des hommes corrompus cette femme seroit trop facile à séduire; souvent sa vertu ne tiendroit qu'aux occasions, dans ce siècle philosophe

il lui faut une à l'épreuve. Il faut qu'elle sache d'avance et ce qu'on lui peut dire et ce qu'elle en doit penser." *Emile*, p. 731.

40. *Emile*, English trans., p. 352. "Femmes de Paris et de Londres, pardonnez-le moi, je vous supplie. Nul séjour n'exclud les miracles, mais pour moi, je n'en connois point, et si une seule d'entre vous a l'âme vraiment honnête je n'entends rien à nos institutions." *Emile*, p. 740.

41. *Emile*, English trans., p. 323. "L'Etre suprême a voulu faire en tout honneur à l'espéce humaine; en donnant à l'homme des penchans sans mesure il lui donne en même tems la loi qui les régle, afin qu'il soit libre et se commande lui-même; en le livrant à des passions immodérées, il joint à ces passions la raison pour les gouverner: en livrant la femme à ses désirs illimités, il joint à ces désirs la pudeur pour les contenir." *Emile*, p. 695. Christine Garbe has analyzed the idea of "pudeur" in Rousseau's works from quite another standpoint, that of power relations between men and women. See her "Sophie oder die heimliche Macht der Frauen: Zur Konzeption des Weiblichen bei Jean-Jacques Rousseau," in *Frauen in der Geschichte*, ed. Ilse Brehmer et al. (Düsseldorf: Schwann, 1983), vol. 4, pp. 65–87.

42 . *Emile*, p. 695.

43. *Emile*, English trans., p. 324. "Que de tendresse et de soins ne lui [à la femme] faut-il point pour maintenir dans l'union toute la famille! Et enfin tout cela ne doit pas être des vertus mais des gouts, sans quoi l'espèce humaine seroit bientot éteinte." *Emile*, p. 697. On this point, cf. the editor's (Gagnebin's) note: "Mais pour la femme, Rousseau ne veut pas parler de vertu. Il s'agit de tendresse et de 'goûts.' La femme a une certaine spontanéité pour remplir ses fonctions maternelles et familiales. C'est pourquoi il est si grave, et vraiment contre nature que les femmes ne veuillent plus d'enfants." *Emile*, p. 1632.

44. *Emile*, English trans., p. 373. *Emile*, p. 770.

45. Bovenschen, *Die imaginierte Weiblichkeit*, p. 178.

46. Discourse on Inequality, p. 108. "[I]l s'agit premièrement de pourvoir au nécessaire, et puis au superflu: ensuite viennent les délices, et puis les immenses richesses, et puis des sujets, et puis des esclaves, il n'a pas un moment de relâche. Ce qu'il y a de plus singulier, c'est que moins les besoins sont naturels et pressants, plus les passions augmentent, et, qui pis est, le pouvoir de les satisfaire; de sorte qu'après de longues prospérités, après avoir englouti bien des trésors et désolé bien des hommes, mon héros finira par tout égorger jusqu'à ce qu'il soit l'unique maître de l'univers. Tel est en abrégé le tableau moral, sinon de la vie humaine, au moins des prétentions secrètes du cœur de tout homme civilisé." *Discours*, p. 114.

47. Bovenschen, *Die imaginierte Weiblichkeit*, p. 173. Paul Hoffmann reaches the same conclusion when speaking of woman's "perfection immobile" (*La Femme dans la pensée des Lumières* [Paris: Ophrys, 1977], p. 380). In the final analysis, however, Hoffmann once again comes back to woman's biological

constitution in order to explain this fixation, thus reproducing the thesis of a sex-specific character bestowed by nature (which is the implicit assumption underlying his entire work): "Elle [la femme] n'est concernée que par les devoirs de la vie privée, sauf à donner à ses devoirs un sens non matériel seulement, mais moral. Et les règles de cette morale, elle les peut interpréter à partir de sa vie la plus charnelle" (p. 379). "La vie charnelle," however, appears to me by no means to explain Sophie's education for ignorance and passionlessness. Hoffmann's argument does not go far enough here because he uncritically adopts, rather than rejects, the (still prevailing) dichotomy between moral sentiment and egoistic (i.e., immoral) reason. The specific nature of Rousseau's representation of femininity, however, as I have tried to show, develops via the function he accords reason within his social system and his theory of the history of humanity.

48. *Emile*, English trans., p. 349. *Emile*, p. 736.

49. *Emile*, English trans., p. 372. "Desirez en tout la médiocrité." *Emile*, p. 769.

50. Jean-Jacques Rousseau, *Julie, ou La Nouvelle Héloïse*, in *Œuvres complètes*, vol. 2, pp. 1–793. For Rousseau's ideas on the function of his heroine as a model, see "Seconde Préface de la Nouvelle Héloïse: ou Entretiens sur le roman entre l'Editeur et un Homme de Lettres," in *Œuvres complètes*, vol. 2, pp. 11–30.

51. James F. Jones correctly points out that Rousseau, in giving Clarens an isolated setting, follows a common topos of eighteenth-century utopian literature, but that he also lends it greater verisimilitude than most by not setting his story on a far-off planet. See James F. Jones, *La Nouvelle Héloïse, Rousseau and Utopia* (Geneva: Droz, 1977), pp. 54ff.

52. Just as in the *Social Contract* Rousseau conceived of the economic self-sufficiency of a people as the "resurrection of the ideal" of self-sufficient natural man, "which the individual can no longer achieve," Clarens, too, appears to be tied to a vision of a state of nature on a higher plane. See Fetscher, *Rousseaus politische Philosophie*, pp. 237–43. See also Klaus Dieter Schulz, *Rousseaus Eigentumskonzeption* (Frankfurt am Main: Campus, 1980), pp. 58ff.

53. *La Nouvelle Heloïse*, p. 548. "Notre grand secret pour être riches . . . est d'avoir peu d'argent, et d'eviter autant qu'il se peut dans l'usage de nos biens les échanges intermédiaires entre le produit et l'emploi. Aucun de ces échanges ne se fait sans perte, et ces pertes multipliées réduisent presque à rien d'assés grands moyens, comme à force d'être brocantée une belle boëte d'or devient un mince colifichet. Le transport de nos revenus s'évite en les employant sur le lieu, l'échange s'en évite encore en les consomant en nature, et dans l'indispensable conversion de ce que nous avons de trop, en ce qui nous manque, au lieu des ventes et des achats pécuniaires qui doublent le préjudice, nous cherchons des échanges réels où la comodité de chaque contractant tienne lieu de profit à tous deux."

54. Ibid., pp. 550–51. "Ajoutez enfin que l'abondance du seul nécessaire ne peut dégénérer en abus; parce que le nécessaire a sa mesure naturelle, et que les vrais besoins n'ont jamais d'excès. On peut mettre la dépense de vingt habits en un seul, et manger en un repas le revenu d'une année; mais on ne saurait porter deux habits en même tems ni diner deux fois en un jour. Ainsi l'opinion est illimitée, au lieu que la nature nous arrête de tous côtés, et celui qui dans un état médiocre se borne au bien-être ne risque point de se ruiner."

55. Ibid., pp. 556–57. "[C]ontens de leurs fortunes ils [les maîtres de la maison] ne travaillent pas à l'augmenter pour leurs enfans; mais à leur laisser avec l'héritage qu'ils ont reçu, des terres en bon etat, des domestiques affectionnés, le goût du travail, de l'ordre, de la modération, et tout ce qui peut rendre douce et charmante à des gens sensés la jouissance d'un bien médiocre, aussi sagement conservé qu'il fut honnêtement acquis."

56. Ibid., pp. 547–48. "[C]hacun trouvant dans son état tout ce qu'il faut pour en être content et ne point désirer d'en sortir, on s'y attache comme y devant rester toute la vie, et la seule ambition qu'on garde est celle d'en bien remplir les devoirs."

57. Ibid., p. 447. "Ai-je tort, Milord, de comparer des maîtres si chéris à des pères et leurs domestiques à leurs enfans? Vous voyez que c'est ainsi qu'il se regardent eux-mêmes."

58. Ibid., p. 444. "Cependant un moyen plus efficace encore, le seul auquel des vues économiques ne font point songer et qui est plus propre à Mad^e de Wolmar, c'est de gagner l'affection de ces bonnes gens en leur accordant la sienne. Elle ne croit point s'acquiter avec de l'argent des peines que l'on prend pour elle, et pense devoir des services à quiconque lui en a rendu. Ouvriers, domestiques, tous ceux qui l'ont servie ne fut-ce que pour un seul jour deviennent tous ses enfans; elle prend part à leurs plaisirs, à leurs chagrins, à leur sort; elle s'informe de leurs affaires, leurs intérêts sont les siens; elle se charge de mille soins pour eux, elle leur donne des conseils, elle accomode leurs différens, et ne leur marque pas l'affabilité de son caractère par des paroles emmiellées et sans effet, mais par des services véritables et par de continuels actes de bonté."

59. Otto Brunner, "Das ganze Haus und die alteuropäische Ökonomie," in *Neue Wege der Verfassungs- und Sozialgeschichte*, ed. O. Brunner (Göttingen: Vandenhoeck, 1968), pp. 103–27.

60. On the question of emotional transparency and the harmony of interests at Clarens, see Jean Starobinski, *La Transparence et l'obstacle* (Paris: Plon, 1957), esp. p. 104. English trans., *Jean-Jacques Rousseau: Transparency and Obstruction*, trans. Arthur Goldhammer (Chicago: UP of Chicago, 1988).

61. Ibid., pp. 444–45. "On n'a point ici la maxime que j'ai vû regner à Paris et à Londres, de choisir des domestiques tout formés, c'est à dire des Coquins déjà tout faits, de ces coureurs de conditions qui dans chaque maison qu'ils parcourent prennent à la fois les défauts des valets et des maîtres, et se font un

métier de servir tout le monde, sans jamais s'attacher à personne. Il ne peut regner ni honnêteté, ni fidélité, ni zele au milieu de pareilles gens, et ce ramassis de canaille ruine le maître et corrompt les enfans dans toutes les maisons opulentes."

62. Ibid., p. 449. "[O]n n'a rien oublié pour que les vices des villes ne pénétrassent point dans une maison dont les maîtres ne les ont ni ne les souffrent."

63. This becomes apparent in a list of guests to the estate: "Si l'on voit rarement ici de ces tas de desœuvrés qu'on appelle bonne compagnie, tout ce qui s'y rassemble interesse le cœur par quelque endroit avantageux, et rachette quelques ridicules par mille vertus. De paisibles campagnards sans monde et sans politesse; mais bons, simples, honnêtes et contens de leur sort; d'anciens officiers retirés du service; des commerçans ennuyés de s'enrichir; de sages meres de famille qui amenent leurs filles à l'école de la modestie et des bonnes mœurs; voilà le cortège que Julie aime à rassembler autour d'elle. Son mari n'est pas faché d'y joindre quelquefois de ces avanturiers corrigés par l'âge et l'expérience, qui devenus sages à leurs dépends, reviennent sans chagrin cultiver le champ de leur pere qu'ils voudroient n'avoir point quitté. Si quelqu'un récite à table les évènemens de sa vie, ce ne sont point les avantures merveilleuses du riche Sindbad racontant au sein de la mollesse orientale comment il a gagné ses trésors: Ce sont les rélations plus simples de gens sensés que les caprices du sort et les injustices des hommes ont rebutés des faux biens vainement poursuivis, pour leur rendre le goût des véritables." Ibid., pp. 553–54. No cross section of French society is assembled here; rather, it is the "drop-outs," disappointed by urban and court life, who can appreciate the rural isolation. Only this purification, "l'âme saine," makes a life at Clarens possible. James F. Jones also notes the significance of lived experience for the decision of those assembled at Clarens to settle there. For him, however, their sole motive is a passive endurance of fear and misfortune, compared to which Clarens seems a consoling place. "[O]ne enters Clarens only after experiencing some type of anguish and only after being in need of the absolute solace that utopia can offer." Jones, *Rousseau and Utopia*, p. 50. His analysis ignores the moment of conscious critique of social conditions.

64. See Michel Gilot and Jean Sgard, eds., *Le Vocabulaire du sentiment dans l'œuvre de J.-J. Rousseau* (Geneva: Slatkine, 1980). "Cette opposition entre les passions naturelles et les passions factices se retrouve dans toute son œuvre: les signes positifs et négatifs, les adjectifs mélioratifs et péjoratifs s'y distribuent selon que les passions découlent de l'amour de soi ou de l'amour propre" (p. 350), or "Tout l'effort de Rousseau vise à retrouver dans le sentiment un élément premier, fondamental. Le sentiment 'vrai,' 'pur,' 'naturel,' 'droit,' se reconnaitra à la force de l'adhésion intérieure" (p. 10).

65. *La Nouvelle Héloïse*, p. 450. "[E]lle [Julie] soutient, que de l'amour ni de l'union conjugale ne resulte point le commerce continuel des deux sexes. Selon elle la femme et le mari sont bien destinés à vivre ensemble, mais non pas de la même manière; ils doivent agir de concert sans faire les mêmes choses. La vie

qui charmeroit l'un seroit, dit-elle, insuportable à l'autre; les inclinations que leur donne la nature sont aussi diverses que les fonctions qu'elle leur impose; leurs amusemens ne different pas moins que leurs devoirs; en un mot, tous deux concourent au bonheur commun par des chemins différens, et ce partage de travaux et de soins est le plus fort lien de leur union."

66. Ibid., p. 662. "Ton sistême se vérifie très-bien ici. Les deux sexes gagnent de toutes manières à se donner des travaux et des amusemens différens qui les empêchent de se rassasier l'un de l'autre et font qu'ils se retrouvent avec plus de loisir. Ainsi s'aiguise la volupté du sage: s'abstenir pour jouir c'est ta philosophie; c'est l'épicuréisme de la raison."

67. Ibid., p. 372. "L'amour est accompagné d'une inquiétude continuelle de jalousie ou de privation, peu convenable au mariage qui est un état de jouissance et de paix."

68. Ibid., pp. 372–73. "Il n'y a point de passion qui nous fasse une si forte illusion que l'amour; on prend sa violence pour un signe de sa durée; le cœur surchargé d'un sentiment si doux l'étend, pour ainsi dire, sur l'avenir, et tant que cet amour dure on croit qu'il ne finira point. Mais au contraire, c'est son ardeur même qui les consume; il s'use avec la jeunesse, il s'efface avec la beauté, il s'éteint sous les glaces de l'âge, et depuis que le monde existe on n'a jamais vû deux amans en cheveux blancs soupirer l'un pour l'autre."

69. Ibid., pp. 493–94.

70. Ibid., p. 495. "Mes succès m'encouragerent, et je voulus tenter votre guérison."

71. Ibid., p. 511. "A la place de sa maitresse je le force de voir toujours l'épouse d'un honnête homme et la mere de mes enfans: j'efface un tableau par un autre, et couvre le passé du présent. On mène un Coursier ombrageux à l'objet qui l'effraye, afin qu'il n'en soit plus effrayé. C'est ainsi qu'il en faut user avec ces jeunes gens dont l'imagination brule encore quand leur cœur est déjà refroidi, et leur offre dans l'éloignement des monstres qui disparoissent à leur approche."

72. Jean Starobinski expressly points to Wolmar's "therapeutic" function. "Das Rettende in der Gefahr," *Neue Rundschau* 92, 3 (1981), 42–71; quotation on pp. 56–57. Starobinski emphasizes that, through Wolmar's intervention, the two lovers do indeed remain virtuous until the novel's end, but they are not "cured," as Julie's deathbed declaration of love demonstrates. I have not dealt here with this aspect of the failure, the crack constantly running through the Clarens principle.

73. *La Nouvelle Héloïse*, p. 664. "Voici la premiere fois de ma vie où j'ai pu vous écrire sans crainte et sans honte. . . . Aurions-nous jamais fait ce progrès par nos seules forces? Jamais, jamais mon bon ami, le tenter même étoit une temérité. . . . J'ai vû votre cœur sensible, plein des bienfaits du meilleur des hommes, aimer à s'en pénétrer."

74. Ibid., p. 486. "J'ai cru voir l'image de la vertu où je cherchois celle du

plaisir. Cette image s'est confondu dans mon esprit avec les traits de Mad^e de Wolmar, et pour la première fois depuis mon retour j'ai vu Julie en son absence, non telle qu'elle fut pour moi et que j'aime encore à me la représenter, mais telle qu'elle se montre à mes yeux tous les jours."

75. Ibid., p. 487. "Je croyois voir son œil pénétrant et judicieux percer au fond de mon cœur et m'en faire rougir encore."

76. Ibid.

77. Ibid., pp. 677–78. "Quand cette redoubtable Julie me poursuit, je me réfugie auprès de Madame de Wolmar et je suis tranquille; où fuirai-je si cet azile m'est ôté? Tous les tems, tous les lieux me sont dangereux loin d'elle."

78. Ibid., p. 678. "Julie, en vérité je crois avoir deux ames, dont la bonne est en dépot dans vos mains."

79. Ibid., p. 441. When Saint-Preux enters the Elisée he exclaims, "La campagne, la retraite, le repos, la saison, la vaste plaine d'eau qui s'offre à mes yeux, le sauvage aspect des montagnes, tout me rappelle ici ma délicieuse Isle de Tinian."

80. Ibid., p. 471. "[J]e crus voir le lieu le plus sauvage, le plus solitaire de la nature, et il me sembloit d'être le premier mortel qui jamais eut pénétré dans ce désert."

81. Ibid., pp. 473–74. "[D]ans ce lieu seul on a sacrifié l'utile à l'agréable, et dans le reste des terres on a pris un tel soin des plans et des arbres qu'avec ce verger de moins la récolte en fruits ne laisse pas d'être plus forte qu'auparavant. Si vous songez combien au fond d'un bois on est charmé quelquefois de voir un fruit sauvage et même de s'en rafraichir, vous comprendrez le plaisir qu'on a de trouver dans ce desert artificiel des fruits excellens et murs quoique clairsemés et de mauvaise mine; ce qui donne encore le plaisir de la recherche et du choix."

82. Jones, *Rousseau and Utopia*, p. 62.

Chapter Six

1. Choderlos de Laclos, "Discours sur la question proposée par l'Académie de Châlons-sur-Marne: Quels seraient les meilleurs moyens de perfectionner l'éducation des femmes," and "Des femmes et de leur éducation," in *Œuvres complètes*, ed. Laurent Versini (Paris: Gallimard, 1979), pp. 387–434. The third essay (pp. 434–443), which sets up a canon for women's reading, and which was written between 1795 and 1802 for a certain (unknown) "comtesse de Gurson" (see Notes, pp. 1414ff.), is untitled.

2. Ibid., p. 389.

3. Ibid., p. 390. "Ou le mot d'éducation ne présente aucun sens, ou l'on ne peut l'entendre que du développement des facultés de l'individu qu'on élève et de la direction de ces facultés vers l'utilité sociale."

4. Ibid., p. 391. "Partout ou il y a esclavage, il ne peut y avoir éducation."

5. Ibid., p. 420. "Soit force, soit persuasion, la première qui céda, forgea les chaînes de tout son sexe."

6. Ibid., pp. 421–22. "Ces premières vérités connues, elles apprirent d'abord à voiler leurs appas pour eveiller la curiosité; elles pratiquèrent l'art pénible de refuser, lors mêmes qu'elles désiraient de consentir; de ce moment elles surent allumer l'imagination des hommes, elles surent à leur gré faire naître et diriger les désirs; ainsi naquirent la beauté et l'amour; alors le sort des femmes s'adoucit, non qu'elles soient parvenues à s'affranchir entièrement de l'état d'oppression où les comdamne leur faiblesse; mais dans l'état de guere perpétuelle qui subsiste entre elles et les hommes, on les a vues à l'aide des caresses qu'elles ont su se créer, combattre sans cesse, vaincre quelquefois, et souvent, plus adroites, tirer avantage des forces même dirigées contre elles."

7. Georges Louis Leclerc Comte de Buffon, *De l'homme*, ed. Michèle Duchet (Paris: Maspero, 1974), pp. 132–33. "[C]e n'est que parmi les nations civilisées jusqu'à la politesse que les femmes ont obtenu cette égalité de condition, qui cependant est si naturelle et si nécessaire à la douceur de la société: aussi cette politesse dans les mœurs est-elle leur ouvrage; elles ont opposé à la force des armes victorieuses, lorsque par leur modestie elles nous ont appris à reconnaitre l'empire de la beauté, avantage naturel plus grand que celui de la force. . . ."

8. Laclos, "Discours," p. 392. "Se conserver et se reproduire, voilà donc les lois auxquelles la nature a soumis les femmes. Ainsi, pourvoir à leur nourriture personnelle, recevoir les approches du mâle, nourrir l'enfant qui en est provenu et ne l'abandonner que lorsqu'il peut se passer de ses soins, telles sont les impulsions naturelles que les femmes reçoivent. Souvents nos institutions les en éloignent, jamais la nature ne manque de les en punir."

9. Buffon, *De l'homme*, pp. 132–33.

10. Laclos, "Discours," p. 394. "Qui voudra savoir combien est délicieux et fort le sentiment de l'amour maternel, qu'il n'aille pas dans les palais des grands où l'intérêt et la vanité sollicitent seuls la génération; qu'il évite les cabanes des pauvres où la misère l'étouffe quelquefois . . . qu'il fuie les hommes aujourd'hui trop dépravés, mais qu'il consulte les animaux; en est-il un si timide qu'il ne devienne courageux pour la défense de ces petits? un si cruel qu'il ne soit doux et folâtre avec eux? un si volage qu'il ne se fixe à leur donner ses soins? La femme seule consent à se séparer de sons fils . . . mais non; chez elle-même la nature est violée et non pas séduite. Mères sensibles, répondez, qui de vous s'est vu enlever son enfant nouveau-né sans l'arroser de quelques larmes?"

11. Ibid., pp. 398–99. "Le feu de l'imagination qui, dans la société, ne manque presque jamais d'être allumé, soit par la vue d'actions ou de tableaux relatifs, soit par des discours ou des lectures peu chastes, et par les réflexions solitaires qui les suivent, est une cause morale, non moins puissante, pour hâter la nature."

12. I cannot agree with Paul Hoffmann, who considers Laclos' position liber-

tine. The fact that, in Laclos' model, *femme naturelle* does not live in a bourgeois marriage, and that her maternal duties end when it is no longer necessary for her to feed her child, is not, in my opinion, a call to libertinage, as Hoffmann interprets it, but, rather, a result of the biological reductionism described. That it is not based on libertine ideas can be seen in the transfer of *femme naturelle* to the state of society. While gender relations in the state of nature are described as polygamous, and the fact that man and woman part *sans dégoût* whenever they wish (p. 403) is cited as a decisive difference from conditions in the state of society, there is in the image of the *femme parfaitement heureuse*, an attempted synthesis between *femme naturelle* and conditions in the state of society, another *formule*: "ce sera celle, qui . . . parvenue à l'âge des plaisirs, aura trouvé pour époux 'un homme toujours nouveau,' amoureux sans être jaloux, assidu sans être importun" (p. 409). See Paul Hoffmann, *La Femme dans la pensée des Lumières* (Paris: Ophrys, 1977), pp. 539–40.

13. See Madelyn Gutwirth, "Laclos and 'le Sexe': The Rack of Ambivalence," *Studies on Voltaire and the Eighteenth Century* 189 (1980), 247–96; quotation on p. 289. "He never particularises this image, which remains vapid, featureless and empty, exactly like that of a ladies' magazine portrait of female destiny."

14. Laclos, "Discours," pp. 409–10. "Créons à notre gré une femme parfaitement heureuse, autant que l'humanité le comporte; ce sera celle qui, née d'une mère tendre, n'aura pas été livrée en naissant aux soins d'une mercenaire; qui plus grande, aura été élevée sous les yeux d'une institutrice également indulgente, sage et éclairée qui, sans jamais la contraindre, et sans l'ennuyer de ses leçons, lui aura donné toutes les connaissances utiles et l'aura exemptée de tous les préjugés; qui parvenue à l'âge des plaisirs, aura trouvé pour époux un homme toujours nouveau amoureux sans être jaloux, assidu sans être importun; qui, devenue mère à sa tour, aura goûté la douceur de l'amour maternel, sans en ressentir les inquiétudes perpétuelles, souvent suivies d'un affreux désespoir, dont l'imagination sage aura vu fuir sans regret son heureuse jeunesse."

15. Jürgen von Stackelberg, "'L'Amour de la guerre et la guerre de l'amour': Der 'Krieg der Geschlechter' in Laclos' *Liaisons dangereuses*," in *Themen der Aufklärung*, ed. J. von Stackelberg (Munich: Fink, 1979), pp. 129–50; quotation on p. 147. See also his essay "Le Féminisme de Laclos," in *Thèmes et figures du siècle des lumières: Mélanges offerts à Roland Mortier*, ed. R. Trousson (Geneva: Droz, 1980), pp. 282–83. "En effet, Laclos se révèle dans ce traité plus rousseauiste que jamais; avec cette différence que tout ce qu'il dit se réfère à la femme, que Rousseau n'avait pas vue. . . . Laclos nous apparaît comme un continuateur et en même temps un correcteur du système de Rousseau: il remplit la lacune 'féministe' laissée dans l'univers de Rousseau."

16. Stackelberg, "Le Féminisme de Laclos," pp. 285–98. Anne-Marie Jaton, "La Femme des Lumières, la Nature et la différence," in *Figures féminines et roman*, ed. Jean Bessière (Paris: Presses Universitaires de France, 1982), pp. 280–98; quotation on pp. 75–87.

17. Stackelberg, "Le Féminisme de Laclos," p. 284.

18. Laclos, "Discours," pp. 432–33. "[N]'imitez pas surtout ces femmes plus vaines que sensibles qui, satisfaites d'un triomphe passager, ne songent qu'au public et oublient leur amant; femmes injustes, vous vous plaignez d'être bientôt abandonnées par eux, vous les accusez de légèreté; prenez vous à vous-mêmes de cette apparente perfidie; votre figure rieuse et fraiche leur avait fait illusion, votre corps flétri les a détrompé. La figure attire, mais c'est le corps qui retient. L'une est le filet et l'autre la cage; mais l'oiseleur prudent, avant de tendre ses pièges, s'occupe des moyens de conserver la proie qu'il pourra faire; imitez-le dans ses précautions, puis vous songerez à embellir votre figure."

19. Ibid., p. 435. "[U]ne jeune personne qui a de l'esprit et de la figure, et que son rang et sa fortune mettent dans le cas de vivre dans la compagnie la plus distinguée, et même d'y avoir de l'influence."

20. Ibid., p. 443. "Nous espérons en même temps qu'elle y [à la lecture] gagnera un assez bon esprit pour ne jamais montrer ses connaissances qu'à ses amis les plus intimes et pour ainsi dire comme confidence. Enfin nous la prévenons que dans la rivalité du cercle, et pour y obtenir de l'indulgence, elle aura besoin d'y montrer plus de simplicité, à mesure qu'elle y portera plus de mérite."

21. Jaton, "La femme des Lumières," pp. 83–85.

Chapter 7

1. Antoine Léonard Thomas, *Essai sur le caractère, les mœurs et l'esprit des femmes* (Paris: Moutard, 1772), p. 98.

2. Ibid., p. 95.

3. Ibid., pp. 95–96. "[E]lles portent à Dieu un sentiment qui a besoin de se répandre, & qui ailleurs seroit un crime. Avides du bonheur & le trouvant moins autour d'elles, elles s'élancent dans une vie et vers un monde différent. . . . Enfin gênées par-tout, privées d'épanchement avec les hommes par la contrainte de leur sexe, avec les femmes par une éternelle rivalité, elles parlent au moins de leurs plaisirs & de leurs peines à l'Etre suprême qui les voit, & souvent déposent dans son sein des foiblesses qui leurs sont chères, & que le monde entier ignore. Alors se rappellant leurs douces erreurs, elles jouissent de leur attendrissement même sans se le reprocher; & sensibles sans remords, parce qu'elles le sont sous les regards de Dieu, elles trouvent des délices secrettes jusques dans le repentir & les combats."

4. Ibid., p. 99. "[L]a nature attentive, pour conserver les mœurs des femmes, a pris soin elle-même de les environner des barrières les plus douces. Elle a rendu pour elles le vice plus pénible et la fidélité plus touchante."

5. Ibid. ". . . par sa réserve, par cette pudeur qui repousse même ce qu'elle desire, & quelquefois dispute à l'amour ses droits les plus tendres."

6. Ibid., p. 98. "Où est ce caractère tout à la fois touchant & sublime qui ne sent rien qu'avec excès? Est-ce dans la froide indifférence & la triste sévérité de tant de pères? non: c'est dans l'âme brûlante & passionnée des mères. Ce sont elles qui, par un mouvement aussi prompt qu'involontaire, s'élancent dans les flots pour en arracher leur enfant qui vient d'y tomber par imprudence. Ce sont elles qui se jettent à travers les flammes, pour enlever du milieu d'un incendie leur enfant qui dort dans son berceau. Ce sont elles, qui pâles, échevelées, embrassent avec transport le cadavre de leur fils mort dans leurs bras, collent leurs levres sur ses levres glacées, tâchent de réchauffer par leurs larmes ses cendres insensibles. Ces grandes expressions, ces traits déchirans qui nous font palpiter à la fois d'admiration, de terreur & de tendresse, n'ont jamais appartenu & n'appartiendront jamais qu'aux femmes. Elles ont dans ces momens, je ne sais quoi qui les élève au dessus de tout, qui semble nous découvrir de nouvelles armes, & reculer les bornes connues de la Nature."

7. Ibid., p. 100.

8. Ibid., p. 101. "[L]es femmes enfin, pour qui les choses ne sont rien, & les personnes presques tout; les femmes en qui tout réveille un sentiment, pour qui l'indifférence est un état forcé, & qui ne savent presque qu'aimer ou haïr, semblent devoir sentir bien plus vivement la liberté & le plaisir d'un commerce secret, & les douces confidences que l'amitié fait & reçoit."

9. Ibid., p. 102. "[Q]u'est-ce qu'une amitié qui est sur ses gardes, où tous les sentimens sont couverts d'un demi voile, & où il y a presque toujours une barrière entres les âmes?"

10. Ibid., p. 104. "[O]n ne s'associe pas fortement sans de grands intérêts. Et les femmes par leur état même sont vouées au repos."

11. Ibid., p. 103. "Cette amitié est imposante & sévère: pour en bien remplir les devoirs, il faut être capable de parler & d'entendre le langage mâle & austère de la vérité."

12. Ibid., p. 104. "Les hommes en général ont plus les procédés que les graces de l'amitié; & leurs sentimens les plus tendres ne sont pas fort éclairés sur les petites choses qui ont tant de prix."

13. Ibid., pp. 106–7. "Tout les dispose à l'attendrissement de la pitié. Les blessures, les maux révoltent leurs sens plus délicats. . . . Quelle femme a jamais manqué de respect au malheur?"

14. Ibid., p. 110. "Elles [les vertus des femmes] sont dans la vie ordinaire, ce qu'est la monnoie courante en fait de commerce."

15. Ibid., p. 111. "[M]ais on remarque en général que les femmes corrigent ce que l'excès des passions mettoit d'un peu dur dans le commerce des hommes. Leur main délicat adoucit, pour ainsi dire, & polit les ressorts de la société."

16. Ibid., p. 105. "Il faudroit donc peut-être désirer un homme pour ami dans les grandes occasions, mais pour le bonheur de tous les jours, il faut désirer l'amitié d'une femme."

17. Ibid., p. 107. "Je ne prétends point rabaisser l'amour de la patrie. C'est le plus généreux des sentimens; c'est du moins celui qui a produit le plus de grands hommes, & qui a fait naître ces héros antiques, dont l'histoire étonne tous les jours notre imagination & accuse notre foiblesse. Mais si nous voulons décomposer ce ressort, & examiner de près en quoi il consiste, nous trouverons que l'amour de la patrie chez les hommes est presque toujours un mélange d'orgueil, d'intérêt, de propriété, d'espérance, de souvenir de leurs actions ou des sacrifices qu'ils ont fait pour leurs concitoyens & d'un certain enthousiasme factice qui les dépouille d'eux-mêmes, pour transporter leur existence toute entière dans le corps de l'Etat."

18. Ibid., pp. 108–9. "[M]oins dénaturées que nous [les hommes] par les institutions sociales auxquelles elles ont moins de part . . . un homme est plus pour elles qu'une nation; & le jour où elles vivent, plus que vingt siècles où elles ne seront pas."

19. Ibid., p. 106. "Elles ont surtout cette sensibilité d'instinct qui agit avant de raisonner, & a déjà secouru quand l'homme délibère."

20. Pierre Roussel, *Système physique et moral de la femme* (Paris: Vincent, 1775), p. 49. "Seroit-il vrai, comme on l'a dit, que cet instinct précieux, par lequel la nature a pris soin de lier les hommes, s'altère & s'affoiblit à mesure que la réflexion se perfectionne?"

21. Thomas, *Essai*, p. 48. "Quant au moral, tout en elles [les femmes] prend la forme du sentiment: c'est par cette regle qu'elles jugent toujours les choses & les personnes. . . . Cette organisation étoit sans doute nécessaire dans le sexe, à qui la nature devoit confier le dépôt de l'espèce humaine encore foible & impuissante. Celle-ci eût mille fois péri si elle eût été reduite aux secours tardifs & incertains de la froide raison."

22. Ibid., pp. 90–91. "Ainsi dans la société l'art de gouverner est celui de flatter les caracteres, au lieu que l'art de l'administration, est presque toujours celui de les combattre. La connoissance même des hommes qu'il faut dans tous les deux, n'est pas la même. Dans l'un il faut connoître les hommes par leur foiblesse, & dans l'autre par leur force. L'un tire parti des défauts pour des petites fins, l'autre découvre les grandes qualités qui tiennent à ces défauts même."

23. Ibid., pp. 85–86. "L'homme toujours actif est exposé aux orages. L'imagination du Poëte se nourrit sur la cime des montagnes, aux bords des volcans, sur les mers, sur les champs de batailles, ou au milieu des ruines; & jamais il ne sent mieux des idées voluptueuses & tendres, qu'après avoir éprouvé de grandes secousses qui l'agitent. Mais les femmes par leur vie sédentaire & molle, éprouvant moins le contraste du doux & terrible, peuvent-elles sentir &

peindre, même ce qui est agréable, comme ceux qui jettés dans les situations contraires, passent rapidement d'un sentiment à l'autre?"

24. Ibid., p. 85. "Je demanderai si leurs fibres plus délicates ne doivent pas craindre des sensations fortes qui les fatiguent & en chercher de douces qui les reposent."

25. Thomas, *Essai*, p. 85. "Peut-être leur imagination, quoique vive, ressemble-t-elle au miroir qui réfléchit tout mais ne crée rien."

26. Ibid., pp. 86–87. "[O]bligées par leur devoir, par la réserve de leur sexe, par le désir d'une certaine grace qui adoucit tout. . . . Une contrainte passagere allume les passions; une contrainte durable les amortit ou les éteint."

27. Ibid., p. 64.

28. Mme de Miremont, *Traité de l'éducation des femmes, et cours complet d'instruction*, 7 vols. (Paris: P.-D. Pierres, 1779–89), BN R. 23186-23192, Discours préliminaire, vol. 2, p. xviii. "Nous conviendrons ici de l'inutilité des sciences exactes pour les Femmes; mais quelle étude peut mieux concourir, à former l'esprit à la justesse, que cette partie de la Physique fondée sur l'expérience? La brièveté de ces éléments fera voir cependant, que je n'élève pas mon sexe à l'orgueil de prétendre à tout."

29. Ibid., vol. 1, p. v. "L'art d'instruire les Femmes, renferme avec lui le talent de leur plaire. Disons plus; l'art de persuader n'est rien pour elles, si on ne les intéresse. C'est à leur *cœur* qu'il faut parler pour rendre leur esprit attentif." Emphasis added.

30. Ibid., Avertissement, vol. 1, p. xvii: "Ses idées sur les inconvéniens de l'Education actuelle m'ont paru si justes, les moyens qu'elle emploie journellement pour y remédier, si faciles & si bien ordonnés, que je l'ai engagée à entreprendre ce travail. Ce ne fut point la vanité d'écrire qui la détermina, c'est un motif bien plus rare, sa complaisance pour son mari, & peut-être la vue de se former un plan, qui assura sa méthode."

31. Ibid., vol. 1, p. xviii. "J'aime à croire qu'elle a eu besoin de mon expérience; qu'elle s'est fait un plaisir de recourir à mes lumières; liés par l'hymen, plus étroitement unis par le sentiment, cet Ouvrage est celui de deux êtres heureux, qui se sont communiqués âme & pensées: enfant du bonheur, je souhaite qu'il prospere."

32. Mme Espinassy, *Essai sur l'éducation des Demoiselles* (Paris: B. Hochereau, 1764), p. 41; BN R. 23200. "Les sciences . . . seront plûtot un délassement pour votre fille, qu'une étude sérieuse."

33. Ibid., pp. 58–60 passim. "[P]lus le roman est vraisemblable, plus il est dangereux."

34. Mme de Miremont, *Traité*, Discours préliminaire, p. xxi. "[L]es garants & les gardiennes de nos vertus."

35. Ibid., p. xxviii. "[C]es arbitres de l'univers."

36. Ibid., p. xxxix. "[P]our assaisonner leurs plaisirs."

37. Ibid., p. xix. "Les hommes cherchent à devenir meilleurs, à mesure qu'ils deviennent éclairés. Les sciences agissent sur l'esprit, l'esprit à son tour fait mouvoir le cœur."

38. Ibid., p. xxii. "On vit dans ces temps [l'époque de la grandeur de la Grèce & de l'ancienne Rome] plus d'une Spartiate demander, non pas, 'Mon fils est-il vivant?' mais 'avons-nous vaincu?' . . . Une femme s'occupoit alors du salut de la patrie, elle s'intéressoit à sa gloire."

39. Ibid., p. xxx. "Monsieur Rousseau . . . est du nombre de ces hommes célébres dont on desire faire oubler les erreurs."

40. Cited in Elisabeth Badinter, *Emilie, Emilie: L'Ambition féminine au XVIIIᵉᵐᵉ siècle* (Paris: Flammarion, 1983), p. 403.

41. Ibid., p. 401. "Mais plutôt que de lutter contre une société fermée aux femmes, pour les faire accéder aux domaines réservés des hommes, Mme d'Epinay préféra donner à Emilie les armes de l'indépendance intérieure."

42. Ibid., p. 402. "On peut jouir de tous les avantages extérieurs, de grandes richesses, d'une bonne santé et cependant n'être point heureux, car le vrai bonheur dépend de nous-mêmes."

43. Ibid., p. 400. "Faites pour conduire une maison, élever des enfants, pour dépendre d'un maître qui demandera tour à tour des conseils et de l'obéissance, il faut donc que les femmes aient de l'ordre, de la patience, de la prudence, un esprit juste et sain. . . ."

44. Ibid., p. 456. "Les hommes et les femmes, étant de même nature et de même constitution, sont susceptibles des mêmes défauts, des mêmes vertus et des mêmes vices."

Conclusion

1. Jean Ehrard, *L'Idée de la nature en France à l'aube des lumières* (Paris: Flammarion, 1963), p. 417.

2. See, for example, the assessment of Annegret Stopczyk, for whom the leitmotif of philosophical thinking about women consists in "(legitimating) in theory what happened in practice" (p. 344). From such a perspective, the differences between the theories indeed diminish, because they apparently arise not from any scholarly intention, but rather from the masculine fallacy, "that everything is fine the way it is" (p. 345). And because women were never equal to men, no philosopher (with a few notable exceptions)—according to Stopczyk—can imagine it, with the result that, from antiquity to the present day, one can demonstrate an unbroken chain of stereotypical "thought products" which are "simplistic, indeed virtually simple-minded" (p. 344). Following this ahistorical premise, women's studies become a lament on the everlasting inability of men

to listen to reason. Annegret Stopczyk, *Was Philosophen über Frauen denken* (Munich: Matthes & Seitz, 1980).

3. See my essay "Critique of Reason and the Concept of Femininity in the French Enlightenment," in *Re-Reading the Philosophical Canon: Feminist Critique in German*, ed. Cornelia Klinger and Herta Nagl-Docekal (University Park: Pennsylvania State UP, in press).

4. Jean Ehrard, *L'Idée de la nature*, p. 207.

5. If Philippe Sollers could lament the disappearance of "real women" (vraies femmes) over the 570 pages of his novel *Femmes*, and if the book could become a bestseller in France in 1983, this was only partly the aggressive and openly sexist salvo of a patriarch robbed of his claims on power. The other part can be attributed to the feeling (half-baked, because expressed in such an unreflected way) that in emerging from a state of tutelage, women have left behind unfinished business. These abandoned tasks were not always for the satisfaction of male chauvinist needs, but frequently made social life possible in the first place. For Sollers, the experience that women were no longer good hostesses, because they could no longer converse aimlessly (!) already signaled the "Fin de la civilisation." Philippe Sollers, *Femmes* (Paris: Gallimard, 1983), p. 287. English trans., *Women*, trans. Barbara Bray (New York: Columbia UP, 1990).

6. Annie Lambert, "Quelques remarques à propos de certains textes de femmes," in *Lendemains* 25–26 (1982), 149–56; Waltraud Gölter, "Regression oder Träume nach vorwärts," in *Lendemains* 25–26 (1982), 139–48.

Bibliography

Primary Sources

Archambault de Laval, Mlle [Madeleine?]. *Dissertation sur la question, lequel de l'homme ou de la femme est plus capable de constance?, ou La Cause des dames.* Paris: La Veuve Pissot, J. Bullot, 1750 (BN R 24081).

Buffon, Georges Louis Leclerc, Comte de. *De l'homme.* Ed. Michèle Duchet. Paris: Maspero, 1974.

Caffiaux, Dom Philippe-Joseph. *Défenses du Beau Sexe, ou Mémoires historiques, philosophiques et critiques pour servir d'Apologie aux femmes.* 4 vols. in 2. Amsterdam: Aux dépens de la Compagnie, 1753 (BN R 24131–24134).

Cahiers de doléances des femmes en 1789 et autres textes. Paris: Editions des femmes, 1981.

Condillac, Etienne Bonnot de. *Essai sur l'origine des connaissances humaines.* In *Œuvres complètes,* 1821–1822. Rpt. Geneva: Slatkine, 1970.

———. *An Essay on the Origin of Human Knowledge.* Trans. Thomas Nugent. Facsimile with an introduction by Robert G. Weyant. Gainesville, Fla.: Scholars Facsimiles and Reprints, 1971.

Descartes, René. *Discours de la méthode.* In *Œuvres et lettres.* Ed. André Bridoux. Paris: Gallimard, 1958. Pp. 123–79.

———. *Discourse on Method and Other Writings.* Harmondsworth, Eng.: Penguin, 1968.

Diderot, Denis. *The Nun.* Trans. Leonard W. Tancock. Harmondsworth, Eng.: Penguin, 1974.

———. *La Religieuse.* In *Œuvres.* Ed. André Billy. Paris: Gallimard, 1951. Pp. 235–393.

145

————. *Supplément au voyage de Bougainville*. In *Œuvres*. Ed. André Billy. Paris: Gallimard, 1951. Pp. 963–1002.

————. *Sur les femmes*. In *Œuvres*. Ed. André Billy. Paris: Gallimard, 1951. Pp. 949–58.

Diderot, Denis, and Jean le Rond d'Alembert, eds. *Encyclopédie ou Dictionnaire raisonné des sciences, des arts et métiers*. 35 vols. Paris: Le Breton, 1751–80. Rpt. Stuttgart: Frommann, 1966–67.

————. *Encyclopedia: Selections*. Ed. Thomas Cassirer and Nelly Hoyt. New York: Macmillan, 1965.

Espinassy, Mme. *Essai sur l'éducation des Demoiselles*. Paris: B. Hochereau, 1764 (BN R 23200).

Laclos, Pierre Choderlos de. *Des femmes et leur éducation*. In *Œuvres complètes*. Ed. Laurent Versini. Paris: Pléiade, 1979. Pp. 387–434.

Lambert, Madame de. "Avis d'une mère à sa fille." In *Œuvres*. Ed. Robert Granderoute. Paris: Champion 1990. Pp. 95–150.

————. "Avis d'une mère à son fils." In *Œuvres*. Ed. Robert Granderoute. Paris: Champion 1990. Pp. 43–94.

————. "Réflexions nouvelles sur les femmes." In *Œuvres*. Ed. Robert Granderoute. Paris: Champion 1990. Pp. 213–37.

Locke, John. *An Essay Concerning Human Understanding*. Ed. John W. Yolton. London: J. M. Dent, 1971.

Miremont, Anne d'Aubourg de La Bove, Comtesse de. *Traité de l'éducation des femmes, et cours complet d'instruction*. 7 vols. Paris: P.-D. Pierres, 1779–89 (BN R 23186-23192).

Poulain de la Barre, François. *De l'égalité des deux sexes: Discours physique et moral, où l'on voit l'importance de se défaire des Préjugez*. Paris: Chez Jean Du Puis, 1673. Rpt. Paris: Fayard, 1984.

————. *The Woman as Good as the Man: Or, The Equality of Both Sexes*. English trans. London, 1677.

————. *De l'éducation des dames pour la conduite de l'esprit dans les sciences et dans les mœurs*. Paris: Chez Antoine Dezallier, 1674 (BN R 47377).

Puisieux, Philippe Florent de. *La Femme n'est pas inférieure à l'homme*. Traduit de l'anglois. London, 1750 (BN Rés. R 2167).

Raulin, Joseph. *Traité des affections vaporeuses du sexe avec l'exposition de leurs symptômes, de leurs différentes causes et la méthode de les guérir*. Paris: J. T. Hérissant, 1758 (BN Td 85.56).

Rousseau, Jean-Jacques. *Discours sur l'origine et les fondements de l'inégalité parmi les hommes*. In *Schriften zur Kulturkritik*. Ed. Kurt Weigand. Hamburg: Meiner 1955. Pp. 62–268.

————. *A Discourse on the Origin of Inequality*. In *The Social Contract and Discourses*. Trans. G. D. H. Cole, rev. J. H. Brumlett, and John C. Hall. London: J. M. Dent, 1973.

————. *Emile ou de l'éducation.* In *Œuvres complètes.* Ed. Bernard Gagnebin and Marcel Raymond. Paris: Gallimard 1969. Vol. 4, Pp. 241–868.

————. *Emile.* Trans. Barbara Foxley. London: J. M. Dent, 1957.

————. *Julie, ou La Nouvelle Héloïse.* In *Œuvres complètes.* Ed. Bernard Gagnebin and Marcel Raymond. Paris: Gallimard 1969. Vol. 2, Pp. 1–793.

————. *Julie or the New Eloise.* Trans. Judith H. McDowell. University Park: Pennsylvania State UP, 1987.

Roussel, Pierre. *Système physique et moral de la femme, ou Tableau philosophique de la constitution, de l'état organique, du tempérament, des mœurs et des fonctions propres au sexe.* Paris: Vincent, 1775 (BN Tb¹²3).

Thomas, Antoine Léonard. *Essai sur le caractère, les mœurs et l'esprit des femmes dans les différens siècles.* Paris: Moutard, 1772. Reprinted in A. L. Thomas, Denis Diderot, Madame d'Epinay, *Qu'est-ce qu'une femme?* Ed. Elisabeth Badinter. Paris: P.O.L., 1989. Pp. 49–161.

Women in Revolutionary Paris, 1789–1795: Selected Documents. Trans. and Ed. Darline Gay Levy, Harriet Branson Applewhite, and Mary Durham Johnson. Urbana: University of Illinois Press, 1979.

Secondary Sources

Abensour, Léon. *La Femme et le féminisme avant la Révolution.* Paris: Ernest Leroux, 1923. Rpt. Geneva: Slatkine, 1977.

Albistur, Maïté, and Daniel Armogathe. *Histoire du féminisme français: Du moyen âge à nos jours.* 2 vols. Paris: Edition des femmes, 1977.

Alcover, Madeleine. *Poulain de la Barre: Une aventure philosophique.* Paris: Papers on French Seventeenth-Century Literature, 1981.

Ariès, Philippe. *Centuries of Childhood: A Social History of Family Life.* Trans. Robert Baldick. New York: Vintage, 1962.

Ascoli, Georges. "Histoire des idées féministes en France du XVIᵉ siècle à la Révolution." *Revue de synthèse historique* 13 (1906), 25–27, 99–106, 161–84.

Auburtin, Graziella. *Tendenzen der zeitgenössischen Frauenliteratur in Frankreich. Ein Beitrag zum literarischen Aspekt der weiblichen Identitätsfindung.* Frankfurt am Main: Haag & Herchen, 1979.

Baader, Renate. *Dames de lettres. Autorinnen des preziösen, hocharistokratischen und "modernen" Salons (1649–1689).* Stuttgart: Metzler, 1986.

————. "Die Literatur der Frau oder die Aufklärung der kleinen Schritte." In *Neues Handbuch der Literaturwissenschaft.* Vol. 13, *Europäische Aufklärung,* 3. Ed. Jürgen von Stackelberg. Wiesbaden: Athenaion, 1980. Pp. 79–106.

Badinter, Elisabeth. *Emilie, Emilie: L'Ambition féminine au XVIIIe siècle*. Paris: Flammarion, 1983.

———. *Mother Love: Myth and Reality*. Trans. Roger De Garis. New York: Macmillan, 1981.

Barbier, Antoine Alexandre. *Dictionnaire des ouvrages anonymes et pseudonymes composés, traduits ou publiés en français et en latin*. 2nd ed. 4 vols. Paris: Barrois, 1822–27.

Baxmann, Inge. "Von der Egalité im Salon zur Citoyenne. Einige Aspekte der Genese des bürgerlichen Frauenbildes." In *Frauen in der Geschichte*. Vol. 3, ed. Annette Kuhn and Jörn Rüsen. Düsseldorf: Schwann, 1982. Pp. 109–37.

Bernal, John Desmond. *Science in History*. 3rd ed. 4 vols. Harmondsworth, Eng.: Penguin, 1965.

Bernier, Olivier. *The Eighteenth-Century Woman*. Garden City, N.Y.: Doubleday, 1981.

Berriot-Salvadore, Evelyne. "The Discourse of Medicine and Science." Trans. Arthur Goldhammer. In A History of Women: Renaissance and Enlightenment Paradoxes. Ed. Natalie Zemon Davis and Arlette Farge. Cambridge, Mass.: Harvard UP, 1993. Pp. 348–88.

Bitterli, Urs. *Die "Wilden" und die "Zivilisierten."* Munich: C. H. Beck, 1982.

Böhmer, Ursula. "Konversation und Literatur. Zur Rolle der Frau im französischen Salon im 18. Jahrhundert. In *Die französische Autorin vom Mittelalter bis zur Gegenwart*. Ed. Renate Baader and Dietmar Fricke. Wiesbaden: Athenaion, 1979. Pp. 109–29.

Boulan, Emile. *Figures du dix-huitième siècle: Fontenelle et Madame de Lambert*. Leiden: A. W. Sigthoff, 1920.

Bovenschen, Sylvia. *Die imaginierte Weiblichkeit. Exemplarische Untersuchungen zu kulturgeschichtlichen und literarischen Präsentationsformen des Weiblichen*. Frankfurt am Main: Suhrkamp, 1979.

Braudel, Fernand, and Ernest Labrousse. *Histoire économique et sociale de la France*. Vol. 2 (1660–1789). Paris: Presses Universitaires de France, 1975.

Brunner, Otto. "Das ganze Haus und die alteuropäische Ökonomie." In *Neue Wege der Verfassungs- und Sozialgeschichte*. Ed. Otto Brunner. 2nd ed. Göttingen: Vandenhoeck and Ruprecht, 1968. Pp. 103–27.

Charles-Roux, Edmonde, et al. *Les Femmes et le travail du moyen-âge à nos jours*. Paris: La Courtille, 1975.

Coquillat, Michelle. *La Poétique du mâle*. Paris: Gallimard, 1982.

Crampe-Casnabet, Michèle. "A Sampling of Eighteenth-Century Philosophy." Trans. Arthur Goldhammer. In *A History of Women: Renaissance and Enlightenment Paradoxes*. Ed. Natalie Zemon Davis and Arlette Farge. Cambridge, Mass.: Harvard UP, 1993. Pp. 315–47.

Delon, Michel. "Le Prétexte anatomique." *Revue du XVIIIᵉ siècle* 12 (1980), 35–48.

Delvailles, Jules. *Essai sur l'histoire de l'idée de progrès jusqu'à la fin du XVIIIᵉ siècle*. Paris, 1910. Rpt. Geneva: Slatkine, 1969.

Dieckmann, Herbert. Introduction to Denis Diderot, *Supplément au voyage de Bougainville*. Geneva: Droz, 1955. Pp. i–civ.

Dörner, Klaus. *Madmen and the Bourgeoisie: A Social History of Insanity and Psychiatry*. Trans. Joachim Neugroschel and Jean Steinberg. Oxford: Basil Blackwell, 1984.

Duchet, Michèle. *Anthropologie et histoire au siècle des lumières: Buffon, Voltaire, Rousseau, Helvétius, Diderot*. Paris: Maspero, 1971.

———. "Du sexe des livres: 'Sur les femmes' de Diderot." *Revue des sciences humaines* 168 (1977), 525–36.

Ehrard, Jean. *L'Idée de nature en France à l'aube des Lumières*. Paris: Flammarion, 1970.

Fauré, Christine. *Democracy Without Women: Feminism and the Rise of Liberal Individualism in France*. Trans. Claudia Gorbman and John Berks. Bloomington: Indiana UP, 1991.

———. "Poulain de la Barre, sociologue et libre penseur." *Corpus* 1 (May 1985), 43–52.

Fellows, Otis. "Diderot's 'Supplément' as a Pendant for 'La Religieuse.'" In *Literature and History in the Age of Ideas: Essays on the French Enlightenment Presented to George Remington Havens*. Ed. Charles G. Williams. Columbus: Ohio State UP, 1975. Pp. 229–43.

Fetscher, Iring. *Rousseaus politische Philosophie*. Frankfurt am Main: Suhrkamp, 1981.

Flandrin, Jean-Louis. *Families in Former Times: Kinship, Household, Sexuality*. Trans. Richard Southern. Cambridge: Cambridge UP, 1979.

Fontenay, Elisabeth de. "Diderot gynéconome." *Digraphe* 7 (1976), 28–42.

———. "Pour Emile et par Emile: Sophie ou l'invention du ménage." *Les Temps modernes* 358 (May 1976), 1774–95.

Fraisse, Geneviève. "Poulain de la Barre, ou le progrès des préjugés." *Corpus* 1 (May 1985), 27–45.

———. *Reason's Muse: Sexual Difference and the Birth of Democracy*. Trans. Jane Marie Todd. Chicago: University of Chicago Press, 1994.

Fricke, Dietmar. "Wiedergeburt in Lieben und Schreiben. Weibliche Erzählende Prosa der Renaissance: Jeanne Flore, Hélisenne de Crenne, Marguerite de Navarre." In *Die Französische Autorin vom Mittelalter bis zur Gegenwart*. Ed. Renate Baader and Dietmar Fricke. Wiesbaden: Athenaion, 1979. Pp. 63–76.

Garbe, Christine. "Sophie oder die heimliche Macht der Frauen. Zur Konzeption des Weiblichen bei Jean-Jacques Rousseau." In *Frauen in der*

Geschichte. Vol. 4, ed. Ilse Brehmer et al. Düsseldorf: Schwann, 1983. Pp. 65–87.

———. *Die weibliche List im männlichen Text. Jean-Jacques Rousseau in der feministischen Kritik*. Stuttgart and Weimar: Metzler, 1992.

Geffriaud-Rosso, Jeannette. "Pour une théorie de la femme: Traités et dissertations de 1600 à 1789." In *Etudes sur la féminité aux XVIIe et XVIIIe siècles*. Pisa and Paris: Goliardica, 1984, pp. 163–211.

Gilot, Michel, and Jean Sgard, eds. *Le Vocabulaire du sentiment dans l'œuvre de J.-J. Rousseau*. Geneva: Slatkine, 1980.

Goldschmidt, Victor. *Anthropologie et politique: Les Principes du système de Rousseau*. Paris: Vrin, 1974.

Gölter, Waltraud. "Regression oder Träume nach vorwärts." *Lendemains* 25–26 (1982), 139–148.

Goncourt, Edmond L., and Jules A. Goncourt. *La Femme au 18e siècle*. Paris: Firmin Didot, 1862. Ed. Elisabeth Badinter. Paris: Flammarion, 1982.

———. *The Woman of the Eighteenth Century*. Trans. Jacques Le Clerq and Ralph Roeder, 1927. Rpt., Westport, Conn.: Hyperion, 1988.

Goodman, Dena. "Enlightenment Salons: The Convergence of Female and Philosophic Ambitions." *Eighteenth-Century Studies* 22, no. 3 (Spring 1989), 329–67.

Goulemot, Jean-Michel. "Prêtons la main à la nature." *Revue du XVIIIe siècle* 12 (1980), 97–111.

Gutwirth, Madelyn. "Laclos and 'le Sexe': The Rack of Ambivalence." *Studies on Voltaire and the Eighteenth Century* 189 (1980), 247–96.

Harth, Erica. *Cartesian Women: Versions and Subversions of Rational Discourse in the Old Regime*. Ithaca, N.Y.: Cornell University Press, 1992.

Hassauer-Roos, Friederike. "Das Weib und die Idee der Menschheit. Überlegungen zur neueren Geschichte der Diskurse über die Frau." In *Der Diskurs der Literatur- und Sprachhistorie*. Ed. Bernard Cerquiglini and Hans Ulrich Gumbrecht. Frankfurt am Main: Suhrkamp, 1983. Pp. 421–45.

Hausen, Karin. "Die Polarisierung der 'Geschlechtscharaktere.' Eine Spiegelung der Dissoziation von Erwerbs- und Familienleben." In *Sozialgeschichte der Familie in der Neuzeit Europas*. Ed. Werner Conze. Stuttgart: Klett, 1976. Pp. 363–93. English trans. "Family and Role-Division: The Polarisation of Sexual Stereotypes in the Nineteenth Century—An Aspect of the Dissociation of Work and Family Life." Trans. Cathleen Catt. In *The German Family: Essays on the Social History of the Family in 19th- and 20th-century Germany*. Ed. Richard J. Evans and W R. Lee. London: Croom Helm, 1981. Pp. 51–83.

Hine, Ellen McNiven. "Mme de Lambert and Her Circle: On the Threshhold of a New Age." *Studies on Voltaire and the Eighteenth Century* 116 (1973), 173–91.

Hinterhäuser, Hans. *Utopie und Wirklichkeit bei Diderot. Studien zum "Supplément au voyage de Bougainville."* Heidelberg: Winter, 1957.

Hoffmann, Paul. *La Femme dans la pensée des Lumières.* Paris: Ophrys, 1977.

Honegger, Claudia. *Die Ordnung der Geschlechter. Die Wissenschaften vom Menschen und das Weib.* Frankfurt am Main: Campus, 1991.

Hübener, Wolfgang. "Die Ehe des Merkurius und der Philologie. Prolegomena zu einer Theorie der Philosophiegeschichte." In *Wer hat Angst vor der Philosophie?* Ed. Norbert W. Bolz. Paderborn: Schöningh, 1982, Pp. 137–96.

Hufton, Olwen. *Women and the Limits of Citizenship in the French Revolution.* Toronto: University of Toronto Press, 1992.

Jaton, Anne-Marie. "La Femme des Lumières, la Nature et la différence." in *Figures féminines et roman* ed. Jean Bessière. Paris: Presses Universitaires de France, 1982, pp. 75–87.

Jones, James F. *La Nouvelle Héloïse, Rousseau and Utopia.* Geneva: Droz, 1978.

Klinger, Cornelia. "Das Bild der Frau in der Philosophie und die Reflexion von Frauen auf die Philosophie." In *Wie männlich ist die Wissenschaft?* Ed. Karin Hausen and Helga Nowotny. Frankfurt am Main: Suhrkamp, 1986, Pp. 26–86.

Kohl, Karl-Heinz. *Der entzauberte Blick: Das Bild vom guten Wilden und die Erfahrung der Zivilisation.* Berlin: Medusa, 1981.

Knapp-Tepperberg, Eva-Maria. "Rousseaus 'Emile ou l'Education.' Sexualauffassung und Bild der Frau: Ein Kapitel zur Antinomie des bürgerlichen Freiheitsbegriffs." *Romanistische Zeitschrift für Literaturgeschichte* (1978), 199–223.

Krauss, Werner. "Cartaud de la Villate und die Entstehung des geschichtlichen Weltbildes in der Frühaufklärung." In *Studien zur deutschen und französischen Aufklärung.* Berlin: Rütten & Loening, 1963, Pp. 157–240.

———. *Zur Anthropologie des 18. Jahrhunderts. Die Frühgeschichte der Menschheit im Blickpunkt der Aufklärung.* Munich: Hanser, 1979.

Kriedte, Peter, Hans Medick, and Jürgen Schlumbohm. *Industrialization Before Industrialization: Rural Industry in the Genesis of Capitalism.* Trans. Beate Schempp. Cambridge: Cambridge UP, 1981.

Kryssing-Berg, Ginette. "La Marquise de Lambert ou l'ambivalence de la vertu." *Revue Romane* 17, no. 1 (1982), 35–45.

Lambert, Annie. "Quelques remarques à propos de certains textes de femmes." *Lendemains* 25–26 (1982), 149–56.

Landes, Joan B. *Women and the Public Sphere in the French Revolution.* Ithaca, N.Y.: Cornell University Press, 1988.

Laqueur, Thomas. "Orgasm, Generation, and the Politics of Reproductive Biology." In *The Making of the Modern Body: Sexuality and Society in the Nineteenth Century.* Ed. Catherine Gallagher and Thomas Laqueur. Berkeley: University of California Press, 1987, Pp. 1–41.

Lee, Vera. *The Reign of Women in Eighteenth-Century France.* Cambridge, Mass.: Schenkman, 1975.

Ley, Klaus. "Weibliche Lyrik der Renaissance. Pernette de Guillet und Louise Labé." In *Die französische Autorin vom Mittelalter bis zur Gegenwart.* Ed. Renate Baader and Dietmar Fricke. Wiesbaden: Athenaion, 1979, Pp. 49–62.

MacLean, Ian. "The Woman Question in Early Eighteenth-Century French Literature: The Influence of François Poulain de la Barre." *Studies on Voltaire and the Eighteenth Century* 116 (1973), 65–79.

———. *Women Triumphant: Feminism in French Literature, 1610–52.* Oxford: Clarendon, 1977.

Melzer, Sara, and Leslie Rabine, eds. *Rebel Daughters: Women and the French Revolution.* New York: Oxford UP, 1992.

Mercer, Philip. *Sympathy and Ethics: A Study of the Relationship Between Sympathy and Morality, with Special Reference to Hume's Treatise.* Oxford: Clarendon, 1972.

Nerlich, Michael. *Kritik der Abenteuerideologie. Beitrag zur Erforschung der bürgerlichen Bewußtseinsbildung, 1100–1750.* Berlin: Akademie Verlag, 1977.

Outram, Dorinda. *The Body and the French Revolution: Sex, Class, and Political Culture.* New Haven, Conn.: Yale UP, 1989.

Piau-Gilot, C. "Le Discours de Jean-Jacques Rousseau sur les femmes, et sa réception critique." *Dix-huitième siècle* 13 (1981), 317–37.

Proctor, Candice E. *Women, Equality and the French Revolution.* New York: Greenwood, 1990.

Proust, Jacques. *L'Encyclopédie.* Paris: Colin, 1965.

Reichardt, Rolf. "Bevölkerung und Gesellschaft Frankreichs im 18. Jahrhundert." *Zeitschrift für historische Forschung* 4 (1977), 154–221.

Rieger, Dietmar. "Die französische Dichterin im Mittelalter. Marie de France— die 'trobairitz'—Christine de Pizan." In *Die französische Autorin vom Mittelalter bis zur Gegenwart.* Ed. Renate Baader and Dietmar Fricke. Wiesbaden: Athenaion, 1979. Pp. 29–48.

Rohbeck, Johannes. *Die Fortschrittstheorie der Aufklärung. Französische und englische Geschichtsphilosophie in der zweiten Hälfte des 18. Jahrhunderts.* Frankfurt am Main: Campus, 1987.

Rousselot, Paul. *Histoire de l'éducation des femmes en France.* 2 vols. Paris: Didier 1883.

Sayers, Janet. *Biological Politics.* London: Tavistock, 1982.

Scheffers, Henning. *Höfische Konvention und die Aufklärung. Wandlungen des honnête-homme-Ideals im 17. und 18. Jahrhundert.* Bonn: Bouvier, 1980.

Schulz, Klaus Dieter. *Rousseaus Eigentumskonzeption.* Frankfurt am Main: Campus, 1980.

Seidel, M. A. "Poulain de la Barre's *The woman as good as the man.*" *Journal of the History of Ideas* 35 (1974), 499–508.

Shorter, Edward. *The Making of the Modern Family.* New York: Basic Books, 1975.

Sieß, Jürgen. *Frauenstimme, Männerstimme. Textrelationen in der Brief- und Romanliteratur des 18. Jahrhunderts.* Paderborn: Igel, 1994.

Sollers, Philippe. *Femmes.* Paris: Gallimard, 1983. English trans. *Women.* Trans. Barbara Bray. New York: Columbia UP, 1990.

Spencer, Samia I., ed. *French Women and the Age of Enlightenment.* Bloomington: Indiana UP, 1984.

Stackelberg, Jürgen von. "'L'Amour de la guerre et la guerre de l'amour.' Der 'Krieg der Geschlechter' in Laclos' *Liaisons dangereuses.*" In *Themen der Aufklärung.* Munich: Fink, 1979. Pp. 129–50.

———. "Le Féminisme de Laclos." In *Mélanges offerts à Roland Mortier.* Ed. R. Trousson. Geneva: Droz, 1980. Pp. 280–98.

Starobinski, Jean. *Jean-Jacques Rousseau: Transparency and Obstruction.* Trans. Arthur Goldhammer. Chicago: Chicago UP, 1988.

———. "Das Rettende in der Gefahr." *Neue Rundschau* 92, 3 (1981), 42–71.

Steinbrügge, Lieselotte. "Critique of reason and the concept of femininity in the French Enlightenment." In *Re-Reading the Philosophical Canon: Feminist Critique in German.* ed. Cornelia Klinger and Herta Nagl-Docekal, Pennsylvania State UP, in press.

———. "Qui peut définir les femmes? L'idée de la 'nature féminine' au siècle des Lumières." In *Dix-huitième siècle* 26 (1994), 333–48.

Stopczyk, Annegret. *Was Philosophen über Frauen denken.* Munich: Matthes & Seitz, 1980.

Tomaselli, Silvana. "The Enlightenment Debate on Women." *History Workshop* 6 (1984), 101–24.

Trouille, Mary. "Eighteenth-Century Women Writers Respond to Rousseau: Sexual Politics and the Cult of Sensibility." Ph.D. diss., Northwestern University, 1988.

Weinreb, Ruth Plaut. *Eagle in a Gauze Cage: Louise d'Epinay, Femme de Lettres.* New York: AMS PRESS, 1993.

Woolf, Virginia. *A Room of One's Own.* New York: Harcourt Brace Jovanovich, 1929.

Index

Abensour, Léon, 25
Advantage. *See* Egoism
Alembert, Jean le Rond d', 21
Amour de soi, 61, 65, 78. *See also* Self-
    preservation
Amour-propre, 61, 65. *See also* Egoism
Anthropology, 21–34, 37, 52
    of the sexes, 64–66
Archambault de Laval, Madeleine, 5,
    17–18

Baader, Renate, 19
Body, female, 5, 37, 41–42, 46–48
Barthez, Paul-Joseph, 33, 42
Bovenschen, Silvia, 55
Buffon, Georges-Louis Leclerc, comte
    de, 52, 84–86

Caffiaux, Dom Phillippe-Joseph, 5, 10,
    16–17
Cahiers de doléances, 28
Cartaud de la Villate, François, 60
Character, sex-specific, 4, 88, 99, 103–4,
    109n.5
Child, 4
    and child abandonments, 26
    and childbed, 27, 29
    and childbearing, 25, 43, 97
    and childhood, 86
    and child-rearing, 33, 67

Compassion, 6, 90, 92, 93, 95
Condillac, Etienne Bonnot de, 34
Condorcet, Marie-Jean-Antoine-Nicolas
    de Caritat, marquis de, 54
Corruption, 75. *See also* Depravation

Delon, Michel, 41
Depravation, 61, 69, 77, 87–88. *See also*
    Corruption
    of woman, 64, 68, 87
Descartes, René, 11–12, 36, 37
Desmahis, Joseph, 31–34
Dictionnaire de Trevoux, 27
Diderot, Denis, 8, 21, 26, 28, 29, 44–53,
    91
Divorce, 27
Duchet, Michèle, 45–46, 55

Education, 33–34
    of girls, 56–57, 69–70, 83, 99–104
Egoism, 59, 60–63, 69, 106
Encyclopédie, 21–34
Epinay, Louise d', 103–104
Espinassy, Madame, 100–101

Family, 4, 73
Fénelon, François de Salignac de La
    Mothe-, 18
Fertility, 25. *See also* Reproduction,
    biological

Fetscher, Iring, 66
Fontenay, Elisabeth de, 45–46
Friendship, 77, 93–94

Galen, Claudius, 42
Geschlechtscharakter. See Character,
    sex-specific
Golden Age, 65, 68–71, 77. *See also*
    Nature, state of
Gombaud, Antoine, chevalier de Méré,
    24
Goncourt, Edmond and Jules, 3
Goût. See Taste

Hassauer-Roos, Friederike, 22
Helvétius, Claude-Arien, 43, 54
Hippocrates, 30
Hobbes, Thomas, 61
Hoffmann, Paul, 8
Holbach, Paul-Henri-Thiry, baron d',
    54
Honnête homme, 24–25
Honnête femme, 25–26
Hume, David, 60
Hutcheson, Francis, 60
Hysteria. *See* Vapors

Idleness, 24, 25, 34, 59
Instinct, 39, 86, 92
    animal, 67
    maternal, 87, 96
    of self-preservation, 72
Intellect, 38–40

Jaton, Anne-Marie, 88
Jaucourt, Louis, chevalier de, 25, 27
Jones, James F., 81

La Mettrie, Julien Offray de, 43
Laclos, Pierre Choderlos de, 3, 83–90
Lambert, Anne-Thérèse, marquise de, 5,
    18–20
Learned woman, 15–18, 33, 37, 70, 103,
    106
Lenclos, Ninon de, 70
LeRoy, Georges, 23, 33
Locke, John, 34, 40, 61

Marriage, 27–28, 30, 78
Maintenon, Françoise d'Aubigné,
    marquise de, 18
Mallet, Edmé, 33
Mandeville, Bernard de, 28, 61
Ménuret de Chambaud, Jean-Joseph,
    30
Midwife, 29
Miremont, Anne d'Aubourg de la Bove,
    comtesse de, 100–103
Modesty, 67–68, 91, 93
Monde, 31
Montaigne, Michel de, 93–94
Moral action, 70
Moral decay, 85, 101
Moral feeling, 95
Moral judgment, 33, 60
Moral philosophy, 60
Moral sentiment, 79, 84, 101
Morality, 31–32, 70, 73
    familial, 96, 102
    private, 106
Mother, 33
Mother love, 89, 92, 102
Mother, role of, 4, 26

Nature, state of, 61, 64, 80–81, 84, 86
    96. *See also* Golden age
    and natural law, 75
    and natural pity, 61
Needs, 71
    female, 63
    natural, 56, 75
Nollet, Jean-Antoine, Abbé, 100
Novels, 19, 101

Passions, 56, 69, 76–79
    female, 63, 66, 69, 91–93
    natural, 75
Perrault, Charles, 60
Philosophy of history, 60–70, 87
Physiocrats, 26, 28
Population growth, 26
    policy concerning, 52
Poulain de la Barre, François, 5, 10–14,
    19
Private sphere, 6, 32, 68

Procreation, 51, 52. *See also* Fertility;
   Reproduction, biological
Progress, 33, 84
   of civilization, 71
   of human intellect, 103
Public sphere, 34, 45, 68
Puisieux, Philippe Florent de, 5, 10–11,
   13–16

Querelle des femmes, 5, 6, 103, 108

Rationalism, 11–18, 33, 36, 46
Raulin, Joseph, 47
Religiosity, woman's, 47–51, 91
Reproduction, biological, 26, 43, 51–53,
   92, 97
Res cogitans, 12
Res extensa, 12
Rousseau, Jean-Jacques, 4, 7, 54–82
Roussel, Pierre, 6, 35–40, 42–43, 96

Saint-Lambert, Jean-François de, 34
Salon, 3, 31, 34, 88
Sensations, 46
Self-interest. *See* Egoism

Self preservation, 61, 72. *See also amour
   de soi*
Self-sufficiency, 73
Sensibility, feminine, 95, 97–99
Sensitivity, 20, 38–39, 41, 91
Sensualism, 35–37, 41, 46
Sensuality, female, 28, 31, 52
Shaftesbury, Anthony, 60
Sollers, Philippe, 110n.9, 143n.5
Stackelberg, Jürgen von, 87–88
Superstition, 27, 47, 49
Surgeon, 29

Taste, 57–58, 68
Thomas, Antoine Léonard, 6, 35–40, 90–
   99

Utility, 81

Vapors, 38–39, 44, 47
Virtues, 68
   woman's, 91, 94, 97–98, 101
   man's, 97–98

Woolf, Virginia, 98

Printed in the United States
704000002B